IMAGES OF ENGLAND

SOUTHAMPTON
THE THIRD SELECTION

Souvenir of 1906 SOUTHAMPTON

Souvenir of 1907 From SOUTHAMPTON

IMAGES OF ENGLAND

SOUTHAMPTON
THE THIRD SELECTION

A.G.K. LEONARD

TEMPUS

Frontispiece: These neatly composed postcard souvenirs of
Southampton 100 years ago depict lots of happy ladies and children
set within the outlines of the years 1906 and 1907, flanked by
vignettes of town scenes, historic buildings and views of Netley
Hospital and abbey ruins. The cards were issued by the prolific firm
of J. Welch & Sons of Portsmouth, printed in Belgium by their
delicately coloured 'trichromatic' process.

First published 2006

Tempus Publishing Limited
The Mill, Brimscombe Port,
Stroud, Gloucestershire, GL5 2QG
www.tempus-publishing.com

British Library Cataloguing in Publication Data.
A catalogue record for this book is available from the British Library.

ISBN 0 7524 4003 9

Typesetting and origination by Tempus Publishing Limited.
Printed in Great Britain.

Contents

Acknowledgements

Most of the illustrations in this book are drawn from my own collection of postcards, old photographs and ephemera but others have been provided by kind friends and departments of Southampton City Council.

Thanks are due to the City Art Gallery, Local Collections, Oral History Archive and in particular to the City Archive Service and Special Collections (Local Studies and Maritime History) Library at Southampton Central Library, for research facilities, information, illustrations and assistance readily given by their always helpful members of staff.

For information and/or illustrations I am grateful to John Avery, Gillie Blake and Geoff Watts of the Friends of Southampton Old Cemetery; Ian Abrahams and Jim Brown of Bitterne Local History Society; Nigel Wood and Lingwood Netley Hospital Archive; Jack Candy of the City of Southampton Society; Jack Foley and Eric Bush, the leading experts on the postcards of F.G.O. Stuart.

Grateful thanks for their contributions are also extended to Rodney Baker, John Cooper-Poole, Mrs B. Corlett, Dave Goddard, Keith Hamilton, Dave Juson, John Edgar Mann, Mrs J.E. Neale and Jeff Pain.

I am, as usual, much obliged to Tom Holder for photography and especially indebted to John Cox for his expert technical assistance with illustrations, always most generously given.

If we have inadvertently infringed anyone's copyright in respect of photographic reproduction in these pages, compiler and publisher hope they will be excused.

Postcards published by F.G.O. Stuart feature prominently in this compilation, duly identified as his. Wherever possible, other postcard illustrations are credited to their original photographers and publishers; most of them are included in the survey introducing the first *Southampton* volume in this series.

Introduction

This third selection of over 200 historic images – widely sourced from old photographs, postcards, ephemera etc. – provides evocative pictorial documentation of the pattern of everyday life, services and activities, buildings and the development of the town and port of Southampton from Victorian times to the years between the wars.

This book complements the author's two previous volumes on Southampton in the *Images of England* series, extending coverage of their themes and topics and exploring further aspects of local history, recalling forgotten events and some of the people who contributed to the growth and progress of their town or distinguished themselves in various other ways.

While this third volume aims to present a survey significant in its own right, it should preferably be read in conjunction with its predecessors. In all three volumes the extent of treatment of particular topics has regard to the content of other Tempus books, whose subjects include the history of aviation in Hampshire; Supermarine; R.J. Mitchell; Hampshire County Cricket Club; Southampton Speedway; a compilation by the Bitterne Local History Society and *Port of Southampton* by Campbell McCutcheon.

The introduction to *Southampton, The Second Selection* outlined its early history. Put briefly, from being one of the leading English ports in the Middle Ages, Southampton declined in Tudor times and stagnated until beginning its revival in the 1750s as a spa, sea-bathing and resort town. This new role fostered an expanding service economy, promoting seaborne trade and packet services to the Isle of Wight, Channel Islands and France. They were dislocated by the wars with France in 1793-1815 but Admiralty orders for wooden warships brought profitable contracts to shipyards along the Itchen and Test rivers. The return of peace and the advent of steam propulsion promoted maritime development from the 1820s, signalised by the opening in 1833 of the pier built by the local Harbour Board (established 1803); this was followed by completion in 1840 of the LSWR railway link with London and the construction by a London-based company of a series of open and dry docks, brought into use from 1842 onwards. The port's natural advantages of location and double tides, giving long periods of high water, favoured its rapid growth, catering for steamships and ocean liners of ever-increasing tonnage (see chapter eight), until it could claim pre-eminence as the 'Gateway to the World'.

A few census statistics illustrate the growth of Southampton. Its population doubled between 1750 and 1801, to nearly 8,000, then increased more than threefold over the next four decades to nearly 28,000 in 1841. Railway and docks developments were reflected in further increases, to nearly 47,000 in 1861 and over 60,000 in 1881. Incorporation in 1895 of the expanding western suburbs of Shirley and Freemantle, together with Bitterne Park to the east, boosted the totals to 105,000 in 1901 and 120,000 by 1911.

Another boundary extension in 1920, bringing in the areas east of the Itchen (Bitterne, Itchen, Sholing and Woolston) was reflected in the 1921 census total of over 162,000; this rose to 178,000 in 1931. The post-war population of 190,000 in 1951 increased to 205,000 in 1961; since then, the number living within the city boundary has not greatly altered.

As an international passenger port of increasing significance, with supporting business activities, Southampton flourished through Victorian and Edwardian times and between the two world wars. There was, of course, no 'Golden Age' to look back on because this prosperity was not shared by many of those whose labour contributed to it, much less by those unable to gain regular employment. Class and income differences between rich and poor were much greater than today and the lives of the latter were often short, hard and insecure; seeming acceptance of their lowly position in a class-bound society was often belied by bitter industrial disputes and political controversy.

Nevertheless, a certain degree of nostalgia, as evoked by many of the contemporary illustrations presented in this book, may not be out of place, for the general pattern of life was certainly simpler and its pace less hectic than today. This is most noticeable in terms of traffic in the main thoroughfares, which Edwardian postcards often show as almost empty of motor vehicles but full of people – well-served by electric trams as the prime form of urban transportation, although many still walked between home and place of work.

F.G.O. Stuart

Outstanding among the postcard-publishing photographers documenting the Southampton scene a century and more ago was a Scot, F.G.O. Stuart, who served his adopted town for forty years, until his death in 1923.

Born in 1842 at Braemar, son of a gamekeeper on the Duke of Fife's estate, he was given his splendid name Francis Godolphin Osborne in compliment to the family of the Duke of Leeds, who had a house there. Stuart began his career as a carpenter and maker of wooden cameras in Aberdeen, graduating into professional photography in his twenties. He boldly moved to London a decade later, setting up studios in Upper Norwood and off St Paul's Churchyard. In 1882 he transferred his business to Southampton, initially taking premises in Bedford Place before soon establishing his home and workplace at Nos 57-61 Cromwell Road – near the former 'Dell' ground of Southampton FC.

In the 1890s Stuart contributed many photographs to local guidebooks and other publications, notably the London magazine *Army and Navy Illustrated*, building up a large stock of material on which he drew for the postcards he began publishing in 1901. Initially they were printed in black and white by the A & N magazine publishers Hudson & Kearns Ltd, but from 1903 Stuart issued a long series finely lithographed by the firm of C.G. Roder in Leipzig, whose delicate and realistic colouring did full justice to Stuart's sensitive camera work. In 1911 keen trading competition on cards retailed at one old penny each obliged Stuart to adopt cheaper production in cruder colours. His main numbered series had reached nearly 2,000 when the outbreak of war in 1914 ended his German connection. Subsequent British-printed cards varied in quality.

Altogether Stuart published over 2,500 different cards, including several hundred without serial numbers. He travelled quite widely to photograph their subjects; nearly half his cards were of Southampton and Hampshire scenes, while the others spanned nearby counties and London, with some 300 devoted to shipping.

Although prolific in output, Stuart's business was not large. From 1893 he employed another photographer, Charles Ford – sadly killed in the First World War – and a young assistant, John Butt. Stuart's 'dearly beloved wife Agnes Isabella' died in 1900; their only daughter, Flora, who helped her father, married a local newsagent, Charles Dowson. After Stuart's death in 1923, they carried on the business until 1939, issuing reprints and another seventy sepia photographic cards, mostly of liners and dock scenes, carrying the main series to a final total of 2,181.

Stuart's 1906 advertisements described his pictorial cards as, 'so highly praised by the press and prized by collectors' – even more so today, when examples once sold for a penny can command several pounds. Present-day FGOS collectors have been well served by the painstaking researches of their doyen, Jack Foley, who has compiled a comprehensive checklist, now carried forward by Eric Bush.

One does not need to be a specialist to appreciate the nostalgic appeal of Stuart's postcard photographs. They provide a third of the illustrations in this book, particularly those evoking townscapes and suburban scenes a century ago.

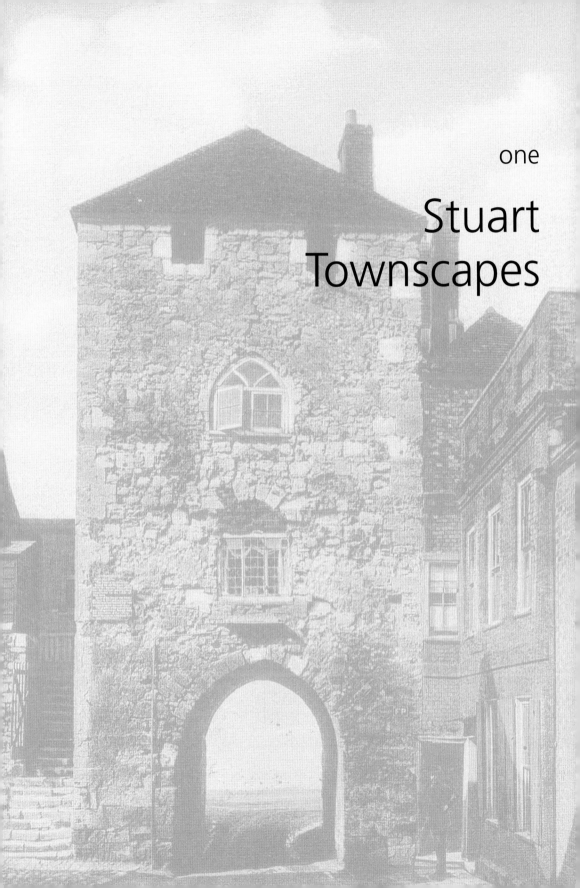

one

Stuart
Townscapes

Stuart pointed his camera down Above Bar around 1900 to show it dominated by the Bargate, the ancient fortified gateway to the medieval walled town – which happily still survives at the heart of the modern city. Depicted in close-up on other Stuart postcards, its north front incorporates the original twelfth-century tower, much extended over the following three centuries. Passages for pedestrians were cut through the side towers in 1764 and 1786.

A later Stuart card reproduced an old engraving of the Bargate, *c.* 1800. Replacing earlier wooden ones, the lead lions still in situ were given to the town by William Lee in 1743. They relate to the medieval romance of Sir Bevis and the virtuous lady Josian. He and his squire Ascupart were depicted on the panels fixed on the buttresses – later taken inside the Bargate. Above the archway, coats of arms of local notable families were put on heraldic shields, *c.* 1700.

The south front of the Bargate has itself changed little since Stuart issued this postcard over 100 years ago. The statue of George III in Roman emperor's costume presented by the second Marquis of Lansdowne in 1809 is flanked by windows forming part of the 1865 restoration project to replace the Georgian sash insertions made to light the upper chamber then used as guildhall, law courts and meeting place. The monarchs' heads placed on the corbels in 1865 were carved in soft stone that has long since eroded into shapeless lumps.

Another Stuart card shows a lively scene in the High Street south of the Bargate, *c.* 1920. Open-topped electric trams ran through the central archway from 1890 until superseded in 1923 by a low-mounted type with domed roof. With the growth of motor traffic, increasing congestion obliged the Council to remove sections of the adjoining town walls and business premises built right up against them, to allow creation of new roadways around the Bargate in 1932-38.

Above: The ancient town walls provided subjects for several Stuart cards, particularly featuring the distinctive arcades. By royal command in the aftermath of the disastrous French raid on a Sunday morning in October 1338, the seaward defences were strengthened by blocking up frontages of merchants' houses on the quayside and making them part of the walls, secured by a series of nineteen arches carrying a rampart walkway. This 1890s photograph shows Haddon & Beavis, coal merchants and ship brokers, occupying a yard beside the surviving 'Norman House' – which then still had a roof.

Above: Two of the original 1900 'Council houses' are themselves now Listed as of historic interest. They stand above the undercroft of a vanished medieval house. Stuart photographed the chamber for a card issued around 1910 highlighting its finely-ribbed vault and hooded fireplace.

Right: Subject of one of Stuart's first batch of German-printed coloured cards depicting Southampton scenes, around 1903, the fourteenth-century Westgate was important for giving direct access to the West Quay, the centre of the port's maritime activities. Henry V's forces passed through it in 1415 en route to the battle of Agincourt; it would also have been used by the Pilgrim Fathers in 1620. The Westgate was defended by a heavy door and double portcullis – removed in 1745. For some 200 years the upper storeys were let by the Corporation as a private dwelling, until 1935, when restoration to a more traditional appearance involved removal of the tiled roof.

Opposite below: A later Stuart card of around 1910 gives another view of the arcades, including part of St Michael's House, a public lodging house built in 1899 as part of a Corporation scheme of slum clearance and redevelopment. It was demolished in 1972.

The Royal Pier Hotel seen to the right of this 1905 Stuart postcard fell victim to German bombing in 1940 but the sturdy stonework of the fourteenth-century Wool House survived. The medieval port had a large trade with Flanders, Italy etc., exporting wool and importing cloth, wine and luxury goods. After this declined in Tudor times the former wool store served various purposes, including housing French and Spanish prisoners, until sensitively refurbished as the city's Maritime Museum, opened in 1966.

'The Old Prison Southampton' – Stuart's caption recalled use of this medieval building as Bridewell and Town Gaol in 1707-1855. Better known as God's House Tower, it took its name from the nearby hospice/almshouses of God's House, long-associated with Queen's College, Oxford. The early fifteenth-century artillery fortifications at the south-east corner of the town wall added a tower and gallery to an older gatehouse. Since 1961 they have a new use as the Museum of Archaeology.

A statue of Prince Albert by William Theed, given to the town in 1876 by Sir Frederick Perkins (five times its mayor), stood beside the tower for thirty years, becoming dilapidated. It was removed in 1907 for fear its shabby condition might offend his grandson, Kaiser William II, on a state visit that year. Left in store, the statue was chanced upon during the First World War by some soldiers, who broke it up in a misdirected act of anti-German patriotism.

These Stuart photographs taken over 100 years ago offer animated views of the High Street, busy with pedestrians, open-top trams and horse-drawn cabs … not a motor vehicle in sight! Beyond the Dolphin Hotel rises the spire of St Lawrence church, an 1842 replacement of its medieval predecessor; it was closed as redundant and demolished in 1925.

Prominent in the right foreground of the scene below are the classical columns of All Saints church, rebuilt in 1792-95 on the pattern of a Greek temple. Bombed in 1940, its site on the corner with East Street was deconsecrated and redeveloped in the 1950s.

Stuart probably took this photograph of Oxford Street in 1907, soon after the refurbished public house at the right had changed its name to the London Hotel. Across the road, beyond the tram headed for Shirley, the former Radley's Hotel was newly converted into offices for the Royal Mail Steam Packet Company, a major contributor to the growth of the port from the 1840s.

Also photographed around 1907, the South Western Hotel is seen still in its Victorian splendour, adjoining the Terminus Station in a seemingly traffic-free location. Originally started as the Imperial Hotel by a private developer in 1865, it was taken over by the LSWR in 1871. This handsome five-storey 'grand hotel' catering for VIP and well-to-do railway and liner passengers was given a seven-to eight-storey extension in the 1920s. Its heyday between the wars ended abruptly in 1939 when it was requisitioned; it never reopened and the building was later converted into offices.

Used in 1906, this Stuart card offers a view down Above Bar Street. Beyond the offices of the weekly *Southampton Times*, a main feature on the east side is the imposing frontage of the old Royal Hotel. This closed in 1919 and after a period of YMCA management gave way in 1922 to a Woolworth store.

In the foreground opposite are the premises of the busy firm of Hunt, Bance & Co. Auctioneers, House & Estate Agents, Valuers & Accident Office and of Toogood & Sons, The King's Nurserymen & Seedsmen.

This Edwardian scene appeared on Stuart postcards going through various editions from 1904 into the 1920s. Its main feature was the 45ft-high clock tower erected in 1899 at the junction of New Road and Above Bar under the bequest of Mrs Henrietta Bellenden Sayers, 'in evidence of her care for man and beast'. The elaborate composition by the architect S. Kelway Pope to provide horse-troughs and drinking-fountains became a popular meeting place, until ever-increasing traffic and the need for road-widening obliged the Council to remove it in 1934 to Bitterne Park Triangle.

Stuart postcards of the early 1920s highlight the changing pattern of traffic in the town's main thoroughfares, where more and more cars pressed ahead of the diminishing number of horse-drawn vehicles – as exemplified in this view of Above Bar. Prominent at upper left is the Palace Theatre, primarily a music hall, an 1898 reconstruction of the former Royal York Pavilion/Palace of Varieties opened in 1872. Bombed in 1940, it was not rebuilt; its site was occupied by the post-war offices of the *Echo*, more recently superseded by major shopping developments.

In a similar view of Commercial Road, little is now recognisable, following the sequence of new buildings initiated in 1928 by the Empire Theatre. Restyled the Gaumont in 1950, it was given a new identity in 1987, as the Mayflower.

Stuart found a good vista around 1906, looking up London Road between the range of shops on the left, towards Carlton Crescent, and the spires of St Paul's church on the right. Erected in 1828, this was the first church outside the old walled town to cater for its developing northern suburbs. It was bombed in 1940 and not rebuilt.

Posted home by a French visitor in 1907, this Stuart card featured the Stag Gates flanking Lodge Road, formerly the entrance to Bevois Mount House. Following housing development of this estate, the site of these pillars was acquired by the estate agent William Burrough Hill. In 1919 he made a Victory gift of these strips of land to the Council for road widening but retained control of the gates, demolished in June that year. He sold the stonework for re-use in East Park and had the carved stags removed to the garden of his house at Bridell Lodge, Regents Park, where they were later buried.

From the 1740s the Corporation arranged the planting of numerous trees along the main approach to the town, passing the Common to make it a veritable avenue. This was much admired in Georgian times by visitors to what was then becoming a spa and residential resort. When Stuart recorded this scene, 100 years ago, The Avenue still enjoyed sylvan tranquillity, with open-topped trams the main form of traffic traversing it.

Even more tranquil and rural was its northern section, depicted in this Stuart view around 1910 captioned, 'The Avenue from Bassett.' The contrast between its emptiness and the constant flow of traffic today could hardly be more striking.

Stuart probably invited this group of girls to pose for his camera on the Common around 1905. First documented in 1228 but likely to date back to Anglo-Saxon times, this area over which burgesses had 'rights of Common' happily survived almost intact, to be designated a Victorian public park. Some 32 acres were taken for a municipal cemetery in 1843-84 but 365 acres (148 hectares) remain as a permanent amenity today.

'Don't you think those trees in the water are lovely – I do' wrote the sender of this Stuart card in 1905. The other lakes and ponds on the Common derive from disused gravel pits e.g. the Cemetery Lake of the 1880s, but the Ornamental Lake with its picturesque island was created by excavation work started in 1888, continuing over several decades.

The Royal Pier was the subject of several Stuart cards from the early 1900s. Officially opened in 1833 by the Duchess of Kent, accompanied by her daughter Princess (later Queen) Victoria, it was erected by the Harbour Board to provide landing places for steamship services. The original timber pier was reconstructed and enlarged in 1890-92 with increased facilities for recreational use, including an ornate pavilion at the pier head for concerts, dances and other entertainments.

Military bands gave concerts in the pavilion and also played marching up and down the pier promenade. Stuart was there to record one in action, with a soldier in the foreground guarding a pile of kitbags. This card was sent to his father in October 1905 by Arthur, writing aboard the troopship *Dilwara*, about to sail to India.

Shown here on one of the last photographic cards continuing the Stuart series into the 1920s, the approach and entrance to the Royal Pier were reconstructed in 1926-27, to an attractive design by Edward Cooper-Poole, the Harbour Board's long-serving engineer and architect. He died in 1935, a few weeks before he would have retired at seventy. Closed during the Second World War, the pier reopened in 1947 but finally shut at the end of 1979.

E. Cooper-Poole had earlier been responsible for the Harbour Board's new offices, officially opened on 8 September 1925 by Admiral of the Fleet Earl Jellicoe of Scapa. Behind it is the floating dry dock, inaugurated by the Prince of Wales on 27 June 1924. The spectacle of a giant ocean liner like the *Berengaria* or *Majestic* elevated above the water always aroused great interest, until this floating overhaul facility was superseded in 1933 by the King George V Graving Dock, itself recently disused.

Stuart's view of the Western Esplanade around 1901 shows it skirting the water, as it did until reclamation works undertaken between the Wars. Beyond the memorial to Mrs Mary Ann Rogers, heroic stewardess of the wrecked steamer *Stella*, is Pickett's yacht and boat building yard. The cannons – Crimean War trophies and old British guns – went for scrap to help the war effort in 1939-40.

Southampton West railway station (depicted on this Stuart card, British-printed after 1914) was built in 1895, replacing earlier ones sited nearer the tunnel carrying the line under the town. It was enlarged and improved in 1934-35 and renamed Southampton Central, becoming simply Southampton after the original 1840 Terminus Station closed in 1966. Major rebuilding then changed its appearance, with the loss of the well-loved 100ft-high clock tower above the 'up' entrance.

Photographed around 1905 by Stuart, who liked to gather local children to add interest to his compositions, the ancient Crosshouse (now Listed and refurbished), recalls the centuries when the Itchen could only be crossed in small boats rowed by the oarsmen of Itchen Ferry village. This 'weatherhouse' was erected in pre-Tudor times to shelter people waiting for them. It was rebuilt in 1634 during the mayoralty of Peter Clungen, who had his initials carved on it, with the date and town arms. The other Cross House behind it was the warehouse of Tagart, Morgan & Coles, timber merchants.

From November 1836 the Itchen could be crossed for a penny on the new floating bridge, a steam-driven cogwheel and chain type of vessel devised by James Meadows Rendel. The Floating Bridge Company operated a series of improved vessels, mostly Northam-built; Stuart photographed one around 1905.

Bridging the Itchen was a key factor in the growth of Southampton and areas to the east. The first bridge was a wooden one, built in 1797-99 by a company of commercial and landed investors whose scheme included new roads linked to it. They charged tolls, as exemplified by this view of the Northam toll-gate approach, from a postcard issued by Rood Bros around 1912. The original timber bridge was replaced in 1899 by a wrought iron one, itself superseded in 1954 by the present concrete structure. The Corporation bought out the Northam Bridge Company in 1929, when it ended toll charges.

A Stuart card of around 1914 offers a nostalgic view across Cobden Bridge towards Bitterne Park. To promote its freehold housing development there, the National Liberal Land Company itself built this bridge in 1883, handing it over to the Borough Council toll-free.

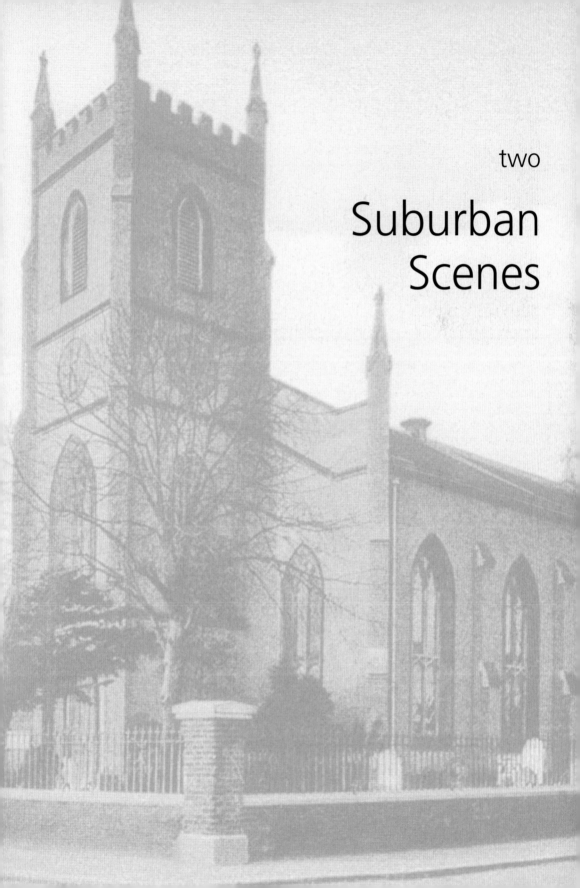

two

Suburban
Scenes

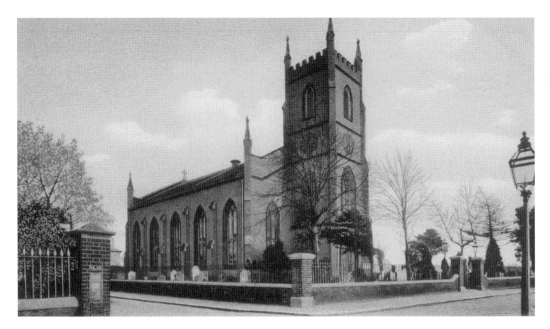

In the early 1800s Southampton prospered as a residential resort, favoured by retired Army and Navy officers and merchants – 'nabobs' and 'planters' who had done well for themselves in the East and West Indies. The town was gradually surrounded by a ring of country houses, 'genteel residences' and smaller dwellings for those who served them. The village of Shirley developed on this basis, its population doubling in twenty years to reach nearly 5,000 by 1861. Subject of a Stuart card around 1905, the church of St James was erected in 1836 to serve the parish of Shirley, created that year by separation from old Millbrook.

Shirley church has changed little in external appearance but the frontages of Church Street leading up to it are now very different from around 1910 when another local photographer gathered this group of children there.

Stuart's idyllic view of around 1903 of part of the then much larger Shirley ponds hardly hints at earlier water-powered industries related to them and the Hollybrook and Tanners Brook streams. Around 1800 the Shirley watermill (mentioned in the Domesday Book) became a tool-making iron factory, then a brewery from the 1850s. The main building housed the Royal Mail ships' laundry in 1900-20; it was demolished in 1959. Another foundry at nearby Freemantle was an important early Victorian engineering and shipbuilding venture, forerunner of Day, Summers and Company, transferred to Northam in 1854.

Regents Park developed from the 1830s as a fashionable area of 'handsome suburban residences' kept exclusive by lodges and gated entrances. Photographed by Stuart around 1905, these had by then outlived their purpose, for the grounds of large old houses were being broken up for smaller-scale house building.

Blighmont, standing in some 50 acres off Waterhouse Lane, was built before 1820 by Admiral Sir Richard Bligh (of Bellevue) for his son Capt. George Miller Bligh. In 1836 his widow married Maj. Nathanial Newman Jefferys of Hollybrook; before settling there around 1842 they lived at Blighmont – here pictured about 1941. Its later owners, around 1900-17, included Nelson Ward, a grandson of the famous Admiral. Thereafter the house was run as a nursing home until demolished in 1963.

Meanwhile, the grounds were being sold off for house building. Blighmont Crescent and Avenue were laid out in the early 1920s, as recalled by this view of the crescent from a postcard sold by George Ayles. He kept the grocer's shop and sub-post office at Testwood Road. The remainder of the Blighmont estate was bought by the British-American Tobacco Co. as the site for its factory opened in 1926.

Nathanial Jefferys and his wife lived at Hollybrook until their deaths in 1873 and 1876. Memorial tablets at St James church recall their benefactions, including the church site and the local 'National' schools – taken over by the Council and replaced in 1912. From the 1880s the Hollybrook estate was sold off piecemeal and in 1902 the Council acquired 47 acres to lay out as the cemetery opened in 1913. In 1910 the Board of Poor Law Guardians bought 13 acres and the house, which it fitted up as a children's home, here shown decorated for the Coronation in 1937. It was demolished in the 1950s when the home closed after children were moved into smaller units or with families.

'The Boys' Dining Room, Hollybrook House' – one of the pre-1914 cards printed in Saxony for the London firm Lofthouse, Crosbie & Co., who specialised in providing publicity cards to schools, hospitals and other institutions.

Contained within its historic boundaries, the population of Southampton itself increased only from 47,500 in 1861 to 65,000 in 1891. The 1901 figure of 105,000 reflected the incorporation in 1895 of Shirley, Freemantle and Bitterne Park. Housing development at Shirley (which continued into the 1930s) promoted the growth of its High Street as a suburban shopping centre, a process only partly illustrated by this Stuart view, c. 1904. Penton's Corn Stores gave way to Lloyds Bank but the Shirley Hotel opposite is still there, recently refurbished.

The electrified service of Southampton Corporation Tramways begun in 1900 greatly helped the growth of Shirley High Street, as shown on this Rood Bros postcard around 1912 after extension of the line in 1911 brought the tram terminus beside the Queen Victoria Jubilee Memorial drinking-fountain and horse-trough. Moved across the road in 1923, it was restored after impact damage in 1970 and re-erected in the Shirley precinct in 1976.

Photographed by Stuart in its sylvan setting around 1905, 'Christ Church, Portswood, commonly called Highfield church' was built in 1847 to serve the parish formerly part of South Stoneham. Complemented by a National School opened in 1849, the church was several times enlarged as the parish grew to, 'no fewer than 3,000 souls' by 1890. Further growth was promoted by electric tram services to Portswood from 1900, taking the population to over 8,000 by 1926.

Another Stuart card of around 1905 offers a view of old Swaythling, looking up the road past the Fleming Arms to the Black Arch – not a vehicle in sight. Prominent in the foreground is The Grange, a Tudor house, for long the home of the Dummer family; it was acquired by the Council in 1965 and demolished in 1974.

Woodmill made an attractive subject for Stuart postcards, British-printed in black and white in 1903 and colour-lithographed in Germany from 1904. It was then a corn mill, rebuilt after a fire in 1820 but earlier it had indeed been a woodworking mill.

Walter Taylor (1734-1803) was an enterprising Southampton carpenter who, initially with his father of the same name (died 1762) and afterwards on his own, developed machine tools for sawing, boring and turning the components for standardised mass production, with great speed and accuracy, of wooden blocks and pulleys for naval ships – halving their weight and reducing friction. Taylor's other patented inventions included circular saws and improved pumps.

Starting before 1758 in workshops at Westgate and later in Bugle Street, Taylor moved his activities in 1770 to a water mill he established at Weston (now Mayfield Park). When its small stream proved inadequate for his expanding operations, he transferred them to Woodmill about 1780 and enlarged the mill, to employ over 100 men on profitable Admiralty contracts. The Royal Navy demand for blocks was immense; a warship required well over a thousand of various types for rigging, gun tackles and other uses. Taylor also set up branch factories on the Thames and engaged contractors. T. Skelton's *Southampton Guide* of 1798 offered an admiring account of Woodmill, where:

> Mr Taylor has erected a curious manufactory of ship-blocks etc., from which his Majesty's dockyards are supplied with all kinds of blocks, from the largest made use of in a first-rate man of war, to the smallest wanted for boats ... the dexterity with which these works are carried on will at once astonish and delight the beholder. Mr Taylor has a patent from the Crown for the security of his invention and we are happy to hear that he is amply remunerated for his ingenuity.

Taylor's large payments from the Admiralty ended when he lost his contract in 1803, the year of his death, when block-making was intensified at Portsmouth dockyard, using improved machines devised by Marc Isambard Brunel – whose offer of collaboration the Taylors had previously declined.

Later owners of Woodmill resumed flour-milling, with a bakery added between the wars. In 1957 the then disused premises were bought by the Council to be given a new use as a schools' sailing and canoeing centre.

'Lances Hill, Bitterne, near Southampton' is the caption to this postcard, one of a series issued by G. Whitfield Cosser, a photographer in business at Hanover Buildings in 1902-05. The name recalled David Lance, who had done well with the East India Co., trading to China as well as India; he had Chessel House built in 1797 and took a leading part in the Company of Proprietors of Northam Bridge and Roads.

Before the gradient was reduced by road works in the 1920s and 1950s parts of Lances Hill were very steep; logs were kept at the roadside for drivers to wedge behind the wheels of their vehicles to give their horses a well-deserved rest.

The toll-gate on Bitterne Road was several times relocated to prevent evasion as new side roads were laid out. It is here shown beside Juniper Road around 1905. After Bitterne was incorporated into the borough in 1920, the Council acquired the Bridge company and ended toll collection on 16 May, 1929.

One of Stuart's best-known postcard photographs is this tranquil village scene around 1904 at Bitterne – later to become a traffic 'black spot'. In the foreground is the pound for stray animals, across the road from the parish church and its associated schools. Consecrated in 1853, the church of the Holy Saviour was built largely at the expense of its first vicar, Revd Henry Usborne, and his sister. The schools erected in 1856 and 1897 and their various later additions were later demolished in 1983, following the opening of the new schools in 1978 on the Brownlow House site.

Flanking the church is another centre of Bitterne village and community life, the Red Lion Hotel, photographed around 1900. Dating from the 1860s, modernised in the 1990s, it continues as a prominent feature of the pedestrian precinct, complemented by the cherished Bitterne Lion.

Lion Place in High Street, Bitterne, was initially a terrace of four shops, built in 1844. It was given a distinctive identity by a stone lion, placed centrally on the parapet. Just visible in front of the chimney stack in this postcard of around 1905, it remained there after Lankester & Crook rebuilt the end shop and added two more frontages in 1891 to open a branch of their County Supply Stores. When all these properties were scheduled for demolition to make way for the by-pass, the lion was carefully removed in 1982, to be refurbished and re-erected in 1987 on a plinth near the Red Lion Hotel. Bitterne Local History Society has adopted it as its emblem.

Another postcard shows a relaxed rural scene around the horse trough at the top of Lances Hill, soon after it was put there early in 1906, through a local public subscription initiated by Lady Amy MacNaghten, widow of the former owner of Bitterne Manor House. In 1988 it was moved into the modern shopping precinct, preserved as part of Bitterne's heritage.

Above: In 1882 the National Liberal Land Co. bought 317 acres of Bitterne Manor Farm and began laying out its Bitterne Park freehold housing estate. Road names exemplified its political identity; Bridge and Avenue both honoured Richard Cobden (1804-65), the great free trade advocate. The Edwardian elegance of Cobden Avenue, looking along to the Congregational church (erected 1902), is nicely depicted in this postcard distributed around 1907 by C.J. Bealing.

Below: Among others memorialised by Bitterne Park road names is Sir Joseph Whitworth (1803-87), an enterprising mechanical engineer who developed a range of instruments and tools achieving great accuracy, including artillery. He later merged his Manchester firm with that of the inventor and ordnance manufacturer, Sir William Armstrong. This Stuart card, used in 1907, shows Whitworth Road partially built, with a group of children adding 'human interest' to the scene.

Bitterne Manor, on the site of the Roman settlement of Clausentum, passed from the Bishops of Winchester into various private ownerships. From around 1850 the house was the home of Sir Stuart MacNaghten (1815-95); recalled by local road names, he was a lawyer and long-time chairman of the Southampton Dock Co. He made Victorian additions to the house – shown here in around 1890, with Lady MacNaghten seated in the garden. Her daughter Letitia continued to live there until 1939. Badly damaged by bombing in 1940, Bitterne Manor House remained derelict until acquired in 1950 by the distinguished architect Herbert Collins, who had it rebuilt to provide fourteen attractive flats.

Bitterne Park Triangle developed as a suburban shopping centre, shown here on a Rood Bros postcard used in 1923 – eleven years before today's landmark, the Sayers clock tower, was re-erected here.

Above: Captioned 'Midanbury Castle, Bitterne Park', this 1921 postcard shows the picturesque lodge at the entrance drive to Midanbury House – another 'country house' estate created in the late eighteenth century. The castellated tower, archway and house in Regency Gothic style replicated Humphrey Repton's design for Blaise Castle, Bristol. Midanbury House was left empty before 1914 and demolished around 1930 after T. Clark & Son had bought the estate for house building; the lodge gave way to the Castle Inn a few years later.

Below: Jesus chapel, Pear Tree Green – featured on a Stuart postcard around 1907 – dates from 1620. The first English church built since the Reformation, it was erected at the expense of Capt. Richard Smith to serve the sparsely populated area east of the Itchen, from which people found it difficult to get to the mother church of St Mary's across the water. As the eastern suburbs grew in Victorian times it was enlarged and supplemented by new churches at Sholing, Woolston and Weston in the 1860s.

Above and below: A guidebook of 1802 noted that, 'William Chamberlayne Esq. is now erecting an elegant mansion on a delightful spot commanding pleasant views'. Weston Grove was sited in the area of today's Archery Road/Swift Gardens, in grounds extending eastward along Weston Lane to Wright's Hill. To take a carriage drive around his estate, Chamberlayne had arched bridges erected over Weston Lane – depicted here on Stuart postcards of 1906. The upper arch above, built in 1802, was demolished in 1931; the lower arch (below) dating from 1816, was removed in 1948. It stood near the old Sun Hotel, recently closed.

Chamberlayne, descended from a Norman family accompanying William the Conqueror in 1066, served Southampton as MP from 1818 until his death in 1829 and was also chairman of the company supplying the town's original gas lighting.

In 1854 Col. Robert Wright bought 35 acres at the eastern end of the Weston Grove estate and there built Mayfield House. In 1889 this estate was bought by Granville Augustus William Waldegrave, third Baron Radstock. On the death of his son, unmarried, in 1937, Mayfield – shown here as a recuperation centre for wounded soldiers during the First World War – was acquired by Southampton Corporation to become a public park. The twenty-three-bedroom mansion was used to accommodate homeless families during and after the Second World War; it was demolished in 1956.

Miller's Pond, Sholing, provided an attractive subject for Stuart's camera around 1903. Even then, there was little trace of a water mill but the pond was valued as a good place for watering horses as well as a 'beauty spot'. More recently, local conversation efforts have helped preserve it from proposed development.

Used in 1906, this Stuart card presents the view up Portsmouth Road to be seen coming ashore from the Floating Bridge. On the left, beyond the waiting room and the Woolston Coffee and Refreshment Tavern, was the headquarters of the 2nd Volunteer Battalion, the Hampshire Regiment. Across the road, beyond the toll house and the Cliff Hotel (closed in the 1980s and converted into flats) a row of shops led up to the Presbyterian church.

St Mary's Presbyterian church, depicted on another Stuart card around 1907, was built in 1876. Many of its early members were from the workforce of Thomas Ridley Oswald, who came with him when he moved his shipbuilding operations from Wearside to Woolston in 1875. The church closed in 1971 when it was sold for site redevelopment as a supermarket.

A novel subject for a Stuart postcard around 1905 was the old seaweed hut on Weston Shore. Revd G. W. W. Minns, vicar of Holy Trinity church, Weston, thought it sufficiently noteworthy to contribute this contemporary account to the Proceedings of the Hampshire Field Club:

> This curious shelter, erected by the fishermen of the village, stands within a few feet of the high water mark on the shore between Woolston and Netley. It covers an area about 25ft by 14ft. Some piles driven in the ground protect the walls and transverse beams of oak support the roof. It is composed entirely of seaweed so closely matted together that the interior presents a smooth surface and is impervious as a wall. The exterior is renewed from time to time by a few loads of seaweed which the fishermen pile on as required. The interior, which measures 18ft by 10ft, was used as a receptacle for spars and fishing gear, in days when there was no road along the shore and such things could be deposited in safety. At present it serves merely as a shelter and rendezvous for the village 'salts'. This primitive construction is marked on an old Admiralty chart bearing the date 1783 but is of much more ancient origin.

There were, of course, stories of the hut being used by smugglers to store kegs of spirits, until they could be taken away at night. Weston, mentioned in an Anglo-Saxon charter of around AD 1000, was formerly an isolated fishing village, well situated for such activities.

For centuries the seaweed hut served local fishermen who regularly 'thatched it', until oil in the sea killed off the seaweed and industrial development spoiled local fishing. Only the Cozens family kept an interest in the hut, which became dilapidated during the 1940s. Barbed wire and corrugated iron ruined its picturesque appearance but failed to stop it being damaged. Voices were raised in favour of repair and preservation but the Corporation regarded it as private property and disclaimed responsibility. Further vandalism made the hut unsafe for local children: a Council bulldozer was sent to demolish it on 4 August 1967. Five months previously, the opening of the Seaweed Inn 200 yards away memorialised this distinctive feature of old Weston – which had been incorporated into Southampton in 1920, along with Woolston, Sholing, Itchen and Bitterne.

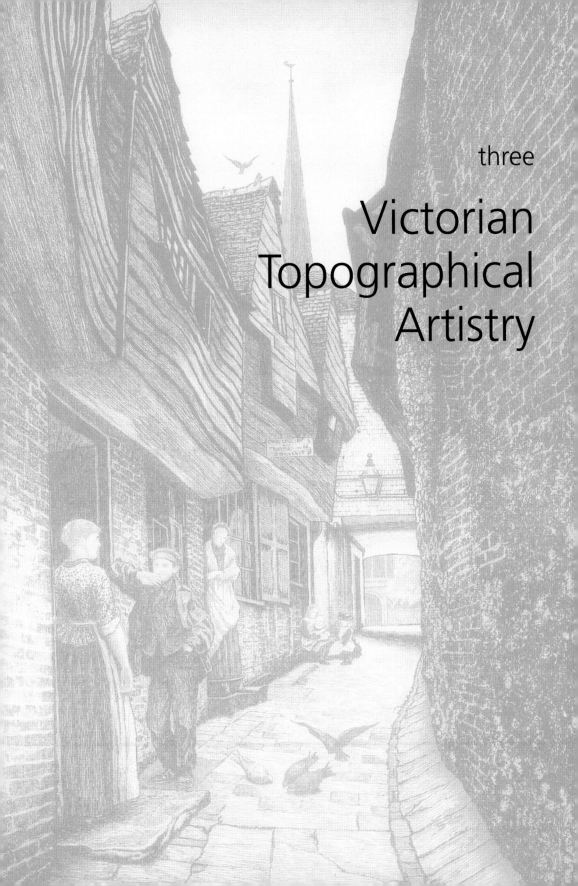

three

Victorian
Topographical
Artistry

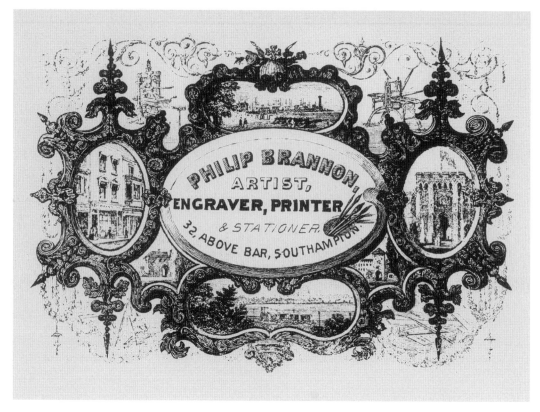

George Brannon (1784-1860) was a successful self-taught artist and engraver who produced a series of illustrated guidebooks on the Isle of Wight that went through many editions. He was assisted by his sons – Alfred (1815-93), who continued the business, and Philip (1817-90), who extended his talents and interests, moving in 1845 to Southampton, where he lived and worked until 1863.

He operated from various addresses; in 1849 he had a shop at No. 32 Above Bar, as featured on his trade card, illustrated above. He then described himself as 'artist, engraver, printer and stationer'; later he could add 'architect, engineer, cartographer, sculptor and inventor', for he was truly a man of many parts, radical views and prolific imagination – although sadly lacking the commercial capacities profitably to apply his far-ranging ideas.

Quickly identifying himself with Southampton, Brannon compiled illustrated guides, notably *The Picture of Southampton* and *Stranger's Guide*, often reprinted from 1850 onwards. He also produced visitor's companions to Netley Abbey, Bournemouth and Dorset. His steel engravings and town maps were complemented by drawings and watercolours e.g. the impressive panoramas of Southampton in Roman, Tudor and Victorian times, now in the City Art Gallery.

Brannon – himself a staunch Unitarian – was architect for the church of the Saviour in London Road, acclaimed in 1860 as 'the cheapest church in Great Britain'; he provided it with an original sound amplification system. This church was bombed in 1940 and Brannon's elaborate 1861 memorial to Richard Andrews was dismantled as unsafe in 1971, but his pioneering reinforced concrete bridge over the River Axe (1877) still stands. Brannon conceived a host of schemes as diverse as fire-resistant and 'healthy' buildings and forms of aerial propulsion and navigation, some of which he patented.

After going bankrupt in 1862, he left Southampton, to spend the next decade back on the Isle of Wight, working as a surveyor to the Shanklin Local Board of Health and engaging in building developments. From the 1870s he lived in the London area, still busily occupied as artist and theoretician. His motto for life was, 'leave the world better for you having lived in it.'

Brannon applied his artistry to enhance this depiction of the Royal Victoria Spa and Assembly Rooms, framed by plentiful foliage and graced with a fashionable gathering. In his *Picture of Southampton* he commended the rooms and rated the Spa as furnishing, 'one of the finest chalybeate waters in the kingdom' but by 1850 Southampton had outlived its time as a resort and was expanding as a maritime and commercial centre.

More realistically, another Brannon engraving reflected changes brought in the 1840s by railway and docks developments, preceded in 1836 by the steam-powered 'floating bridge' crossing of the Itchen. This superseded the historic role of the Itchen Village ferrymen and extended eastwards the influence of Southampton on its future suburbs. Perhaps the men sitting beneath the tree outside the Royal Oak Inn were discussing the changing scene. The old inn in Hazel Road was rebuilt in the late 1890s and destroyed by German bombing in 1940.

Above and below: The Common and the Avenue gave Brannon full scope for sylvan exuberance
in these views 'drawn, engraved, printed and published' by him, *c.* 1849. On the edge of the
common is the inn then officially styled The Southampton Arms but always popularly known as
The Cowherds. It dates from a 1762 replacement of the cottage previously occupied by the town
official employed to look after the animals of citizens having rights of pasture on the common.

Seen through the trees at the right of Brannon's view of the Avenue is the then new Avenue
House. On the corner with Rockstone Place, completing its development by the architect
S.E. Toomer in 1840, this solid Beaulieu brick house had a succession of private tenants until taken
over in 1865 by the Ordnance Survey, to become its 'Director General's House'. After the OS
moved to Maybush in 1969 this Grade II Listed building stood empty until refurbished in 1986 as
prestige offices.

Above: Brannon's delight in picturesque leafy scenes, enhanced in perspective, found full expression in this view of Regents Park around 1850. In early Victorian times this future western suburb of Southampton was favoured by builders of country houses and villas, as here idealised by Brannon. Before the end of Queen Victoria's reign some of their grounds were already in the process of redevelopment, with roads laid out across them for rows of smaller houses.

Below: Brannon's use of perspective to heighten actual dimensions is evident in this engraving titled 'Interior of the Antient Town Hall over the Bargate.' This upper chamber was used for various municipal purposes from medieval times. It served as the guildhall until the building of the new Audit House/Council chamber in the High Street in 1773 and continued in use as a courtroom until transfer to the new Civic Centre in 1933.

In its tree-girt rural location, Jesus chapel, Pear Tree Green, provided an attractive subject for this Brannon engraving around 1848. It may be compared with Stuart's photograph of sixty years later (see page 40). The tree at the right then still raised its ageing gnarled trunk.

Complementing his view of the chapel, Brannon also depicted the eponymous old pear tree on the Itchen Ferry village green. Supposed to date from Queen Elizabeth's time, it still existed in 1901, when the vicar, Revd T.L.O. Davies, wrote of it as, 'now in extreme old age … but not sunk yet'. In fact there were then two pear trees on the green, as shown in Brannon's engraving, c. 1850. Fears of the imminent demise of the old one had prompted Mrs Preston Hulton to plant a new one beside it. Both trees must have died by 1928, when the Corporation provided a replacement, itself renewed in 1939; this was destroyed during the war. A pear tree was returned to the green in December 1951, planted at the end of the Festival of Britain year by the mayor, Alderman Mrs M. Cutler.

Above left and right: This 1890 etching of Blue Anchor Lane is the first in a series of twelve in *Vestiges of Old Southampton* by Frank McFadden, a handsome large volume published by H.M. Gilbert. It depicts the ancient passage between St Michael's Square and West Quay – named from the sign of an old inn. Complementing it is an etching dated 1891, looking along Simnel Street, another alley harking back to medieval times; its flour name probably derives from its location in the bakers' quarter of the town.

The City Art Gallery holds thirty-three examples of McFadden's work – twenty-nine prints of his topographical etchings (including the twelve from *Vestiges of Old Southampton*) and four portraits in oils of municipal worthies – but it does not seem to have information about the artist himself. His biography is simple enough; he died on 17 April 1933, in his seventy-eighth year, having spent most of his working life as an engraver with the OS. Unmarried, he lived throughout at a house called Clovelly, No. 16 Avenue Road, which was the McFadden family home from 1865 or earlier. His father, John McFadden, set the pattern of working for the OS followed by three (possibly four) sons. The elder McFadden died shortly before the 1891 census recorded his widow, Lucy (sixty-five), 'living on her own means' with bachelor sons Rowland (forty-five), William (thirty-seven) and Frank (thirty-four). The first two were identified as OS employees but Frank was described as 'artist, etcher, sculptor'. He may then have been seeking an independent career but in 1901 he was recorded as an engraver at the OS, where brother Rowland had become superintendent engraver.

Most of Frank's etchings and paintings were done during the years 1880-1900. His pictures of old Southampton were highly regarded by contemporaries. Three of his oil paintings – depicting the Bargate, Westgate and St Cross, Winchester – were exhibited at the Royal Academy in 1889-92; their present whereabouts are unknown.

This McFadden etching of 1891 centres on the Old Tower Inn at the corner of Bargate Street and Western Esplanade. The inn and a group of old wooden cottages abutted Arundel Tower – the north-west corner of the town's defensive wall, named after Sir John Arundel, royal governor of the castle in 1377-79. The inn was rebuilt in 1899, as the Old Arundel Tower Hotel. Its demolition around 1968 revealed that this had been partially supporting the shell of the historic tower, which needed under-pinning to make it secure.

McFadden's picture of Above Bar and the north front of the Bargate presents a somewhat idealised scene of late Victorian leisured gentility, a decade before the Corporation started running electric trams through the centre of the town, under the central arch of the Bargate.

This page: In the mid-1880s McFadden was involved with St Mary's Church of England Young Men's Association. He provided some spirited engravings to illustrate the programmes of its athletic meetings held in the Deanery grounds or in the local church school.

His cover design for the Amateur Athletic Meeting held on 26 July 1886 showed fashionably dressed spectators watching two runners straining to outpace each other.

A range of gymnastic activities were also featured on this programme, around a version of his ingeniously contrived monogram of the letters SMYMA – the initials of the St Mary's Young Men's Association.

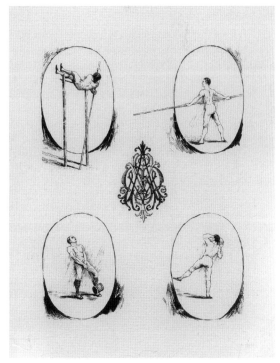

Most of St Mary's young men were also footballers, playing for the team established in November 1885, when its first match resulted in a 5-1 victory over Freemantle. The side flourished and from 1888 developed separately from the church to become the leading club in the region, styled Southampton St Mary's, then from 1897 simply Southampton FC – still generally known as the 'Saints'.

Frank McFadden painted this picture of the side that on 29 March 1890, won the Hampshire FA Junior Cup for the third successive year. Rediscovered at The Dell in the 1990s, it was put on display in the bar of the Supporters Club. On 19 May 2001, during celebrations after the last match at The Dell prior to transfer to the new St Mary's Stadium, the painting was removed by over-enthusiastic souvenir-takers … but returned undamaged a few days later.

McFadden produced his own Christmas cards, in designs combining vignettes of old Southampton scenes. This one includes a view of Tudor House as newly restored for Mr W.F.G. Spranger, which dates it as probably 1902.

Above and next pages: This 110-year-old watercolour offers an unusual view of the roofs of buildings abutting the east side of the Bargate and town wall, as they did until demolished in 1932 for the first phase of creating the traffic circus around the Bargate.

The painting is one of sixty-five done in 1896-97 by William Marshall Cooper (1833-1921) to record scenes of the old town before many were swept away by slum clearance and other redevelopment. He was personally commissioned to provide such pictorial documentation by Southampton's 'Grand Old Man', William Burrough Hill (1845-1941), who purposefully concerned himself with the heritage and public affairs of his native town. Cooper's evocative watercolours formed a significant part of Hill's collection of 228 illustrations of 'Antient Southampton' which he displayed at the Philharmonic Hall in Above Bar in 1898-1909. When obliged to vacate it, he persuaded the Corporation to buy the entire collection for £700.

Cooper's paintings have since been on show only occasionally, because of their sensitivity to light, but thirteen were authentically reproduced in each of the City Council's 2006 and 2007 calendars. These say Cooper was commissioned by the borough surveyor — a risible confusion about the name of William Burrough Hill, who was indeed a building surveyor but in a private professional capacity.

According to the calendars, 'little is known about the artist except that he had previously worked as a surveyor in New Zealand' — even though the Council has owned his watercolours for nearly 100 years! Research has established that William Marshall Cooper was born on 18 March 1833 at Doncaster, into a large North Country family of Quakers. In 1865 he went out to New Zealand (following his younger brother Thornhill Cooper, who settled there and made a name for himself as painter and photographer, living to reach 100 in 1940) and for ten years worked as a government surveyor in Westland, South Island. He painted numerous watercolours of geographical and geological features; the Museum of New Zealand has a score of them and more are preserved in several other New Zealand art galleries and libraries.

Cooper headed the list of artists contributing to the New Zealand presence at the great Centennial Exhibition at Philadelphia in 1876. Soon afterwards, he moved to work in New South Wales, becoming surveyor of public parks in 1883. He left with a gratuity at the end of 1887. How he spent his early retirement years is unknown but he is recorded living on the Isle of Wight in January 1893, when he made a single-sentence will in favour of his wife Annie. She was twenty-three years his junior, destined to outlive him by thirty-one years; their family comprised at least two sons, mentioned in reports of her funeral in 1951. From 1895 the Coopers lived at Wroxall, near Ventnor. They were closely involved with St John's church there. Following his death, aged eighty-eight, on 20 March 1921 (leaving an estate of £963 to his widow), W.M. Cooper was commemorated by two inscribed memorial windows.

Curiously, he does not seem to have painted any of the Island subjects favoured by other artists – perhaps prevented by illness or injury from using his brushes there. However, his highly productive period in 1896-97, resulting from his fortunate contact with W.B. Hill, enabled him to make his own distinctive contribution to Southampton's artistic heritage.

Above: Dated 17.4.96, this Cooper painting of St Michael's Square centres on the Pineapple Inn, in the group of buildings soon afterwards removed for the erection of a municipal lodging house – itself demolished in 1972. *Left:* another Cooper watercolour, dated 23.4.96, depicts Old Silk Shop Yard, off Simnel Street – harking back to the local industry introduced by French Protestant émigrés after 1685.

Above: A view down Simnel Street to the water beyond the West Quay offered an attractive prospect for another Cooper painting.

Below: The artist's depiction of the upper chamber of the building now the Tudor Merchant's Hall following its restoration by the Council in the 1970s. It originally stood in St Michael's Square, erected around 1400 for the town's fish and cloth markets. In 1634 the Corporation sold the building to Alderman Exton, who re-erected it on its present site, as his own warehouse. Set against the town wall, incorporating the sentry walk along the ramparts, it became known as the Guard Room and later as the 'banqueting hall' after it was leased in 1725 to the Marrett family of Westgate House. The old sedan chair featured in Cooper's painting is preserved in Tudor House Museum.

W.M. Cooper painted this view of picturesque old Westgate House only months before it was acquired by the Corporation and demolished in 1898 for extension of the roadway from Western Shore to the pier and docks. The old house incorporated part of the town wall, which had to be reinstated.

Tudor House was opened in 1912 as Southampton's first Council museum, after the Corporation had bought the property from Mr W.F.G. Spranger for £4,500 – about half what this practical philanthropist had spent on it. Cooper's painting shows the frontage as it was in the 1890s, before Spranger initiated thorough-going restoration in 1900-01, to give a seemingly authentic Tudor appearance to the building which dated back to about 1500. The full story is told in the booklet *The Saving of Tudor House* (Paul Cave Publications Ltd for the City of Southampton Society).

four

Selling, Making and Serving

Above and below: In the 1840s Philip Brannon found a profitable outlet for his talents in providing eye-catching trade cards for many of the town's fashionable shops and High Street traders. His designs ranged from compositions of delicate lettering and depictions of shop frontages to elaborate evocations of services offered.

G.C. Wilkinson, 'Fancy Biscuit Baker' at No. 166 High Street, was advertised by a design in which details of his many products, including 'Dobson's Patent Unfermented Digestive Bread', were set out around the royal coat of arms, while a spirited maritime scene exemplified 'Yachting & Export orders executed on the shortest notice & most reasonable terms'.

For C. White's Wholesale & Retail Glass & China Warehouse, Brannon illustrated in remarkable detail the wonderful variety of ornate objects its proprietor had on display at No. 27 Above Bar.

Above: Brannon featured tiger-shooting in this vivid design showing the furs and skins offered for sale at No. 181 High Street by J. Martin & Co., Wholesale & Retail Furriers. Their services included, 'furs cleaned, repaired, altered and freed from moth in a superior manner'.

Below: A nice arrangement of quadrupeds promoted the services of W.C. Spooner, Veterinary Surgeon and 'author & editor of various veterinary works', who had his 'Infirmary & Forge' in Spa Road, off Above Bar. This was supplemented by a 'branch forge' at Bedford Place, where horses were 'systematically shod so as to preserve the feet in a healthy state or to improve them if diseased … horses examined as to soundness'. Moreover, Mr Spooner was able to declare, 'the diseases of all domestic animals [were] scientifically treated.'

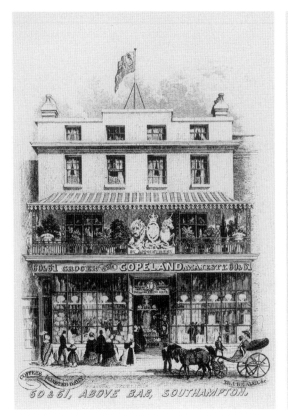

Above left: Mr Copeland's shop at Nos 60-61 Above Bar proclaimed him 'Grocer to her Majesty.' Brannon's trade card gives the impression it was well patronised …

Above right: For Alfred Pegler, 'goldsmith, silversmith, watchmaker & jeweller,' Brannon's card showed his shop at No. 151 High Street, in a vista powerfully dominated by a representation of the elaborate epergne he had created for a tribute to George Laishley, mayor in 1849. That year Alfred Pegler succeeded to the ownership of the family business which his great grandfather Daniel Pegler had come from Blandford in 1794 to establish. Others may have supplied the gentry on credit but Alfred believed that 'ready money is the only true basis of sound trading', so 'all his prices are calculated for cash, from which no abatement can be made.' As well as Jet Goods, i.e. mourning jewellery then in vogue, Pegler made a speciality of electroplating and watches 'of a superior class' for shipping companies and export.

Before the Harbour Board set up its time ball in 1888 on top of God's House Tower, Pegler for many years offered his own facility at No. 151 High Street where 'a time ball in direct communication with the Royal Observatory, Greenwich, is discharged every morning at 10 o'clock, by which unerring standard watches and clocks are regulated.'

A daughter married Eric Wyatt, who took over the business in 1925. After Pegler & Wyatt's premises were blitzed in 1940, the firm merged with former rivals W.L. Parkhouse & Son to form Parkhouse & Wyatt.

Pegler's association with Brannon included his publication from 1866 of a noteworthy little promotional booklet entitled *205 Memorials of Southampton;* these comprised wonderfully detailed minute engravings, all 205 on a single folding sheet less than A4 size.

Pegler's public services included chairmanship of the Red Funnel steamship company in 1881-92.

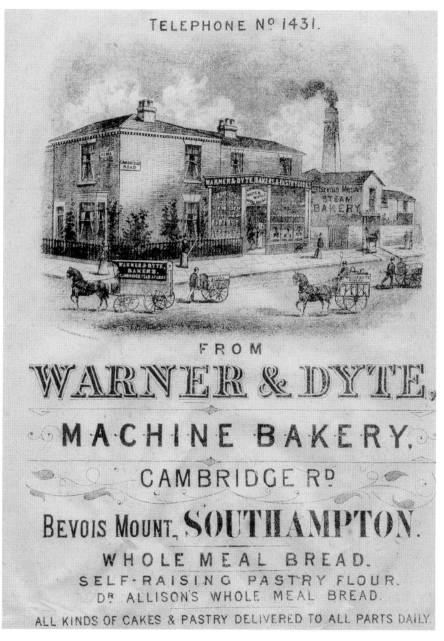

TELEPHONE Nº 1431.

FROM

WARNER & DYTE,

MACHINE BAKERY,

CAMBRIDGE RD

BEVOIS MOUNT, SOUTHAMPTON.

WHOLE MEAL BREAD.

SELF-RAISING PASTRY FLOUR.

DR ALLISON'S WHOLE MEAL BREAD.

ALL KINDS OF CAKES & PASTRY DELIVERED TO ALL PARTS DAILY.

They don't print paper bags like they used to ... This century-old example of advertising artistry, measuring about 5in x 10in, would have been used for a few cakes or pastries rather than the loaves produced by the Warner & Dyer machine bakery. The finely detailed engraving shows the Bevois Mount Steam Bakery (in action with smoking chimney!) and the adjoining shop at Alma House, on the corner of Cambridge and Padwell Roads. In the foreground are featured the horse-drawn van, cart and hand barrows that 'delivered to all parts daily' for the business that operated there from the early 1880s until 1914.

The bakery has long since given way to modern housing but the substantial corner property has found a new role, adapted as offices.

Left: Looking up East Street around 1912, the view is dominated by the mass of All Saints church – rebuilt in 1792-95 in classical style, bombed in 1940. At the left is the sign of Hipps Ltd, tailors; opposite them are the premises of John J. Carter & Sons Ltd, steam dyers and cleaners, and the Southampton Vacuum Cleaner Co. Between them and the Brewery Bar is the Premier Penny Bazaar, then closed.

Below: As Southampton grew during Victorian times, the pattern of town centre retailing beyond the main High Street/Above Bar axis gradually changed, to cater more for the mass of lower income customers. The Premier Penny Bazaar – shown here on an advertising card colour-printed in Germany around 1910 – informed them 'Every Article One Penny; No Other Price; 100,000 Articles always in stock … Walk in and out as you please, you need not buy.' Perhaps too many people followed the latter advice, for B.A. Gale & Co. traded in East Street for only a few years around 1908-12. By 1913 their Penny Bazaar had been taken over by Marks & Spencer.

Above: James Bailey of Chapel Street, Bitterne, traded as dairyman, fruiterer and greengrocer. He drew his milk supply fresh from the 'home farm' of Moorlands, an estate of 120 acres until sold for housing development in 1919. This picture of around 1910 is a reminder of the days when milk was delivered to the housewife's door, transferred from the churn into pint or quart measures and then poured into the customer's own jugs.

Below: The enterprising Mr Lankester opened his first grocery shop in 1855 at Obelisk Road, Woolston. Extended and improved from the 1890s onward, the premises shown here became the headquarters of an expanding chain of branches serving a wide area east of the Itchen. In 1890 Samuel Crook was taken into partnership; after Lankester retired in 1901 he continued the business as Lankester & Crook Ltd, which later involved further generations of the Crook family. From four in the 1880s, L. & C. branches grew to ten by 1910 and later to fifteen. On the basis of 'the best possible goods at the lowest cash prices', L. & C. steadily extended the range of household and other goods stocked, making their County Supply Stores an early combination of local convenience and mini department stores. In changed circumstances L. & C. ceased general trading in 1981 but continued as a property company.

Above: By the early 1900s the Colonial & American Fresh Meat Stores of W. & R. Fletcher Ltd had established a considerable trading presence in Southampton. The 1908 directory listed thirteen Fletcher shops in the town, with others at Woolston and Eastleigh. Posed here for the camera around 1910 are the man and boy staffing the shop at No. 33 Bedford Place.

Above: Southampton Co-operative Society was set up in 1887 by a group of idealistic young dock workers, to engage in 'fair and honest trading' for the benefit of members and 'to substitute for the competitive system co-operative control of the means of production and distribution.' Starting in a small shop in St Mary Street near the workhouse, it soon moved to premises at No. 37 Melbourne Street, shown here in 1907. Designated No. 1 Branch, this was followed by others opened in 1896-1908 at Freemantle, St Denys, Bitterne Park, Woolston, Shirley and Avenue Road, with a steam bakery in Trinity Road and warehouses in St Andrew's Road.

Right: From its initial thirty-three, Co-op membership grew to nearly 4,000 in 1907, with a turnover of nearly £50,000 and 100 employees. Some posed outside the new Central Store at No. 123 St Mary's Road, opened on March 11 1907 by founder member and long-serving president Robert Seward Pearce (1841-1917). Retired Trinity House pilot, member of Itchen UDC, he was also active in the temperance movement but devoted much of his energies to promoting the principles and practice of co-operation.

This block was later extended and reconstructed in 1933 as a department store. It was absorbed in 1970 into a larger store in Bargate Street, itself closed in 1985, deemed as too small for modern trading conditions.

Opposite below: David Greig, provision dealer and tea merchant, opened shops in Southampton about 1920, first at No. 40 London Road and later at No. 113 East Street – pictured here around 1925 during a Southampton Shopping Week. Standing in the doorway wearing his smart white apron, the manager is flanked by offers of 'fresh eggs 3 for 4d' and tea at 2s 6d per pound. The shop adjoined the Picture Palace, one of the town's first cinemas, which from 1911 to 1930 occupied a converted Baptist chapel.

'Sholing Voluntary Workers – Bread Strike, August 1919' identifies the occasion and purpose of this group in a classroom at Sholing Boys' School. Similar groups operated at Ludlow Road School, St Mark's School, Woolston and the Parish Rooms in Chapel Street, Bitterne. They all sought to organise fair distribution of the limited supply of loaves then being produced by master bakers east of the Itchen whose regular workers had joined others in and around Southampton in going out on strike.

In 1919 several factors combined to fuel feelings of unwonted militancy among workers not usually inclined to strike – ranging from London policemen to local Corporation workers. Post-war inflation and the aspirations of returned servicemen added to the pent-up demands of workers whose cost of living increases had been deferred or only partially implemented.

Negotiations between master bakers and their employees were complicated by continuation of wartime controls on flour and bread prices. The cost of a gallon loaf had remained fixed at 9d since September 1917, when bakers' basic wages were £2 7s a week; they had since risen to £3 on which the Operative Bakers' Union sought an increase of £1, together with abolition of night work. Most master bakers felt unable to meet these claims unless they were allowed to raise the price of a loaf to 10d.

To press their case for a national agreement, Union bakers went on strike from Saturday 2 August. After the Bank Holiday weekend, bread shortages took effect from Tuesday. In the event they lasted only a few days. On Thursday talks began, under the chairmanship of the mayor, Alderman Sidney Kimber, at the Bedford Hotel, between representatives of the master bakers and their striking operatives. These led to the men voting to return to work on 9 August, subject to the employers agreeing to implement the outcome of a national settlement of their claim by arbitration … which soon followed, to end the bakers' dispute.

Evoked with Gallic artistry in the early 1900s, the Le Dansk margarine factory was a notable feature of Northam for nearly seventy years. Son of the man who began production near Paris in 1871 and developed exports to Scandinavia and Britain, Auguste Pellerin moved directly into the British market in 1891, when he opened a purpose-built factory in Princes Street. This had its own LSWR railway connection and was commended for its attractive buildings and hygienic mechanised production lines, using refined animal fats sent from France and milk etc. obtained locally.

Under the management of P. Falck, followed by his son from 1925, the venture flourished, to employ some 200 people by 1930, when it diversified into making specialist cheeses. In 1952 a new refinery and power house were erected at Northam but the factory closed in October 1960, following amalgamation with Mitcham Foods Ltd.

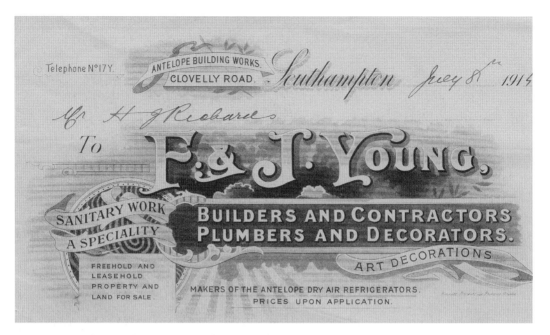

Builders' billheads usually indicate the range of services offered. This example from F. & J. Young identifies them not only as 'builders and contractors, plumbers and decorators' but also as makers of the 'Antelope dry air refrigerators' at their Antelope Building Works in Clovelly Road. In addition, the partners had 'Freehold and Leasehold Property and Land for Sale' – as instanced by this letter of July 1915 succinctly stating, 'In reply to your enquiry our bottom price for the 8 houses is one thousand pounds. They are always let and we get very little trouble with the rent. They are very fair size rooms (6 rooms as usual, 3 up & down)'.

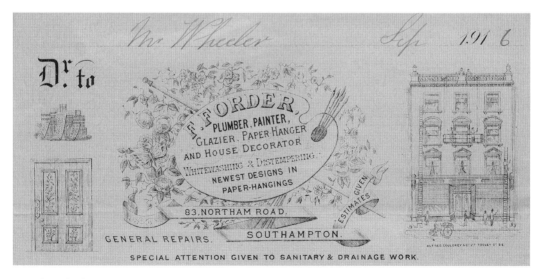

F. Forder, 'plumber, painter, glazier, paper hanger and house decorator' of No. 83 Northam Road, itemised on this sheet work done in September 1916 for a Mr Wheeler at a house in Avenue Road. To wash, repair and distemper ceilings, supply paper at a shilling per roll and paper walls in three rooms cost precisely £1 19s 11d, which was then a reasonable week's wages.

Right: From around 1880 to 1910 the branch post office at Old Shirley was run by Albert Atkins, who for these and many more years kept a grocery shop in Romsey Road (renumbered No. 178 around 1910, near the junction with Redbridge Hill); he is probably the old man standing in front of it, some time in the early 1900s.

Below: A glimpse of Royal Mail service nearly a century ago is given by this much-postmarked envelope of 1912 – back in the days when a labour-intensive organisation provided six town deliveries a day. How hard the postmen tried to deliver the mail is highlighted by this envelope sent on 3 January 1912 from the solicitors Paris, Smith & Randall of Lansdowne House, Castle Lane, to a Mr Watson at No. 8 Anglesea Terrace, Chapel. It was eventually returned to sender marked 'gone away' – but only after zealous efforts to locate the addressee, as indicated by no less than six postmarks while doing the rounds over three days.

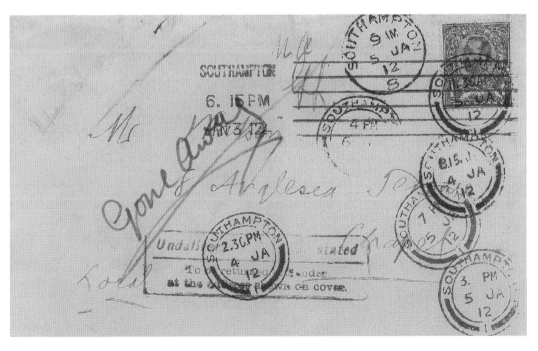

Above: Numerous public houses served townsfolk and visitors during the heyday of the great ocean liners. The Horse & Groom at No. 103 East Street (corner of Canal Walk) was widely known to seamen, not least Americans coming ashore from their 'dry' ships during Prohibition years in the 1920s. Its landlords and bar staff were remarkably long-serving. Mr and Mrs Harry Batten who took over in 1904 (bringing three large stuffed bears as an enduring attraction) were succeeded in 1932 by their daughter, Mrs Gladys Heaton (a teetotaller) who spent her life there until obliged to retire in 1971 when the pub was closed, for retail redevelopment of the site.

Below: Until closed in 1972, the Victoria Inn at Freemantle stood from the 1860s in what was originally Victoria Road, renamed Beatrice Road in 1924 to end confusing duplication. It evidently served the whole community, as evidenced by this pre-1910 photograph of a group posed outside the inn before climbing aboard the horse brake for an outing, probably a day in the New Forest.

Above and below: Victorian Southampton was well-served with hotels, catering for visitors and railway and steamship passengers. Complementing the South Western Hotel and the fashionable establishments in High Street/Above Bar were various smaller hotels near the Terminus station and docks. One of the oldest was Flower's Temperance Hotel in Terminus Terrace, for which Philip Brannon engraved this handsome card in the late 1840s, advertising well-aired beds and meals for a shilling each.

About 1870 James Flower moved what was then styled a 'Family and Commercial Hotel' into larger premises in Queen's Terrace – shown below on publicity postcards produced for his successors around 1910 by F.G.O. Stuart. This hotel closed around 1918, its buildings being taken over by the Missions to Seamen – later redeveloped for a large office block. Through some division of family interests there was also a Flower's Hotel separately continuing in Terminus Terrace from around 1878 until 1939, which must have caused some confusion!

Another 'Family and Commercial' enterprise was Roles Hotel at Nos 37-39 Oxford Street. Its facilities were depicted on multi-vignette publicity cards, colour-printed in Germany. This example was taken to Cornwall by a shipping agent who used it on 24 April 1914 to tell someone that, 'the *Mauretania* arrived at New York last evening'.

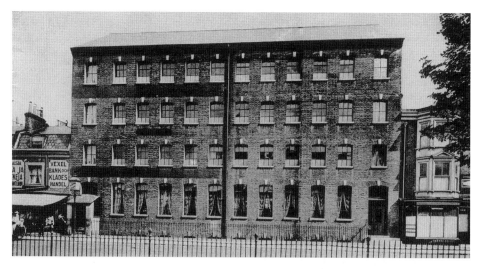

In 1894 John Doling opened his Emigrants' Home in Albert Road to cater for some of the thousands passing through the port. Within a few years he was able to expand it into the large four-storey building, styled the Atlantic Hotel from 1908, shown on his publicity postcards. This example was sent to a mother in London by her son, all kitted up to go somewhere – posted on 5 August 1914, the day after war was declared. Did he get away? The war put an end to the Atlantic Hotel. From 1916 the building was occupied by the British American Tobacco Co.: after 1930 it housed a Ministry of Labour employment exchange for seamen. More recently it was converted into office accommodation.

five

Care for Soul, Mind and Body

"BERNARD"

TO THE GLORY OF GOD,
AND IN MEMORY OF
BERNARD DOMETT NAIRNE
PRIEST,
ENTERED INTO HIS REST,
A.D. 1804
AGED 27 YEARS.

This Stuart photograph, taken around 1905, presents a view of St Mary's church centred on its squat tower, as it appeared from 1884 until funds were raised to add the spire in 1913. The mother church of Southampton, dating back to Saxon days, has been several times renewed: the Norman building was replaced by later structures which proved inadequate, leading to a complete rebuilding to the design of G.E. Street in 1878-84. Badly damaged by German bombs in 1940, the church was reconstructed in stages from 1948, to be completed and reconsecrated on 12 June 1956.

Philip Brannon admired 'the great improvement effecting by enclosure of the churchyard', devoting this engraving to the wall newly erected in 1847, designed by the architect-surveyor J.G. Poole. At the left is the former eighteenth-century church, enlarged in 1833 but demolished in favour of its 1878 replacement. The level of the burial ground had been raised by successive burials through many years, eventually obliging the Corporation to take part of the Common for the municipal cemetery opened in 1846.

Another Stuart postcard depicted St Denys church in a pleasant rural setting, *c.* 1904. Designed by Sir George Gilbert Scott, it was built in 1867 and enlarged in 1889, to serve the Victorian suburb developed in the area taking the name of the patron saint of France – as given to the Augustinian priory established around 1124 by Henry I, for masses to be said in memory of his son Prince William, drowned off the Normandy coast in 1120.

An older church occasioned by the growth of the Victorian town was St Luke's, Newtown, erected in 1853 for the parish newly formed out of St Mary's. Its vicar from 1899 to 1923 was Revd Dr James Trevaskis, a powerful churchman who enlisted a team of able curates, notably Revd Bernard Domett Nairn, who was evidently highly regarded by the parishioners. When he died of enteric fever in October 1904 at the early age of twenty-seven, after nearly four years' service at St Luke's, they subscribed to provide a bell inscribed in his memory – illustrated here from a contemporary postcard.

The small tower then added to the church was badly damaged on 23 November 1940; the bell crashed to the ground but survived intact and in the 1950s was still being rung by a makeshift arrangement outside the church. Does any reader know what happened to it? The church was closed as redundant in 1981 and sold to become a Sikh temple in 1983.

Neatly tree-framed in this Stuart photograph taken a few years after its opening in December 1898, the Avenue Congregational church was a response to the northward expansion of the town's residential suburbs. It was preceded from 1892 by a second-hand 'tin' church which served as a hall until replaced in 1934 by new halls, themselves recently refurbished. Reflecting population changes around it, the Albion Congregational church merged in 1935 with its Avenue offshoot, to which in 1986 was likewise joined St Andrew's Presbyterian church, dating from 1853, to form the present Avenue St Andrew's United Reformed church.

William Booth's preaching in London's East End from 1865 soon promoted The Christian Mission serving other areas; in 1878 this became the Salvation Army. It established a vigorous presence in Southampton from 1881, overcoming initial hostility towards its new-style evangelism through open-air services with a strong musical element. The uniformed Army generally gained respect, particularly for its brass band – subject of this 1909 postcard.

The Southampton branch of the Young Women's Christian Association was launched on 11 October, 1881 in rooms above the offices of J.J. Burnett at No. 2 High Street (beside the Bargate). Initially serving 'young ladies from the principal drapery establishments' by providing classes and a 'quiet retreat', it extended its role to include a residential hostel at No. 22 Portland Street – depicted on postcards of the early 1900s for use by residents. After this property was bombed in 1940, the YWCA occupied temporary premises until the opening in 1955 of Princess Margaret House in Bellevue Road. A prime mover in YWCA activities through several decades was Mrs Amy Louise Burnett, wife of the accountant Ernest George Burnett, who supported her and was also closely involved with the YMCA.

From No. 6 Carlton Crescent Dora wrote on 24 January 1904 to tell Hilda 'have just commenced my second term's work at College'. Hilda was far away in Australia so the two halfpenny stamps Dora put on this much-travelled postcard were not enough and the distant recipient had to pay 3d postage due on it.

Opened in 1903 to accommodate Catholic students attending the teacher training department of Hartley University College, the hostel in Carlton Crescent was a temporary arrangement by the Sisters of La Sainte Union pending the establishment in 1904 of their own residential college for training women teachers.

The religious teaching order founded in France in 1826 extended its work to England in the 1860s. It came to Southampton in 1880, purchasing Archers' Lodge, an old house with several acres of grounds off The Avenue; there the sisters opened early in 1881 their 'superior school for young ladies'.

The Convent High School flourished in larger premises incorporating the original house, as depicted here on one of its own publicity postcards. It was complemented from 1904 by St Anne's secondary day school – into which the CHS was eventually absorbed in the 1960s.

F.G.O. Stuart photographed the three-storey red brick building of the Convent Residential Training College soon after its opening in September 1904. Extra accommodation was provided by acquisition of several nearby houses and later by additional buildings in the 1960s when the college expanded rapidly; it admitted non-Catholic and male students and diversified as a college of higher education offering a range of courses for degrees from Southampton University – into which it was merged in 1997 as its 'New College'.

Depicted on Stuart postcards from 1904, Hartley University College occupied the site of three houses in the High Street previously belonging to Henry Robinson Hartley (1777-1850), an eccentric recluse who bequeathed his inherited fortune of over £100,000 to the Corporation, for contentiously ill-defined cultural purposes. Reduced to only £42,500 by expensive lawsuits and claims, this bequest was eventually applied to building the institution ceremonially opened by the Prime Minister, Lord Palmerston, on 15 October 1862.

Another Stuart card of the early 1920s showed the buildings of what became in 1902 a University College, associated with the University of London. Its move to the first phase of new buildings at Highfield, scheduled for 1914, was delayed until 1919 by the War Office, which accepted an offer to use college buildings as a military hospital during the First World War. Temporary wooden huts then erected served the college through several decades, until large-scale expansion followed the achievement of full university status in 1952.

Above and below: William Capon (*c.* 1480–1550), a scholar and preacher whose numerous appointments included being rector of St Mary's from 1529 until his death, bequeathed £100 to the town for establishing a free grammar school. This was opened in 1554 in a large room in Winkle Street, removing in 1696 to premises at Bugle Street.

In early Victorian times, King Edward VI School languished, actually closing in 1854 for lack of pupils. Reopened in 1860 after the Corporation had extended and improved its accommodation, it thereafter grew steadily, making necessary its move to new buildings erected in 1896 on the Kingsbridge House site, off Havelock Road. These were featured in the early 1900s on a series of publicity postcards, two of which are illustrated here.

In 1920 land off Hill Lane was purchased for use as playing fields and for the erection in 1938 of extensive new school buildings, successively enlarged in recent years.

This metal name plate of Taunton's School from around 1850 was salvaged from a heap of bomb damage rubble during the Second World War. The school was established in 1760 through the bequest of Richard Taunton (1684-1752), a wealthy merchant, alderman and twice mayor of Southampton. He intended it to prepare up to twenty boys to go to sea but it gradually broadened its curriculum and increased its numbers. Outgrowing a succession of rented premises, from 1864 it occupied its own buildings at New Road, rebuilt and enlarged in 1878, 1893 and 1899.

The latest additions to its buildings were acclaimed at the Speech Night of 1899, for which A. Bailey of Form Va designed the programme. The occasion was marked by the presentation of 'his portrait in oils' to Robert Chipperfield, chairman of the endowed schools' governors from 1877 until 1905. A successful chemist, dedicated to public service, he is best remembered for his generous legacy to the Art Gallery.

Developing from the 1900s as a grammar school, Taunton's hopes of transfer to larger new buildings at Highfield were deferred by the First World War and not realised until 1926-27, after the Borough Council had taken over responsibility for the school in 1924. From 1967, Taunton's became a sixth form college. Co-educational from 1978, it merged with the former grammar school for girls and moved to the Hill Lane site in 1994; its Highfield buildings are now part of the university.

A proud day for the School Board, 18 October 1896 saw the laying of the foundation stone at Mount Pleasant by its chairman, Canon John Michael Scannell. Widely respected, he was the parish priest of St Joseph's, 1885-99. His chairmanship exemplified the partnership between board and voluntary schools, working to extend public elementary education from 1871, when Southampton was among the first to establish an elected school board under the 1870 Education Act.

Harmonising the political and religious interests involved, it undertook an impressive building programme to tackle the inadequacies of the patchwork of church, charity and dame schools which in 1870 left entirely uneducated more than half the children of the expanding town. By 1899, when the population of the borough was estimated at 106,000 with about 17,600 children of school age (5-13), the board had provided 11,168 school places – more than double the accommodation of the voluntary schools, which had increased only to 5,134 from 4,418 in 1870.

Mount Pleasant represented 1,230 places in three departments – 510 infants, 360 boys and 360 girls. The board's architect, J.H. Blizard (partner of the celebrated James Lemon) had to overcome severe foundation problems on a site subject to tidal flow; a preliminary contract involved driving 900 piles and creating extensive cellars before the main contractors, H. Stevens & Co., started work. Blizard praised the craftsmanship of their workers, who attended the stone-laying ceremony, at which the banner of the local branch of the Operative Bricklayers Society was prominently displayed.

The schools were officially opened on 10 February 1898, when the chief guest, Sir George Kekewich, permanent secretary of the Education Department in Whitehall, lavishly praised them as 'truly magnificent … most conveniently arranged and spacious'. A notable amenity was the large central hall, 84ft x 40ft. On the following two days some 10,000 people flocked to inspect this £33,000 project; most admired it but in some quarters it was criticised for extravagance.

An imposing clock tower was a feature of the Mount Pleasant complex – not to be repeated in the board's next buildings necessitated by extension of the borough boundary in 1895 to take in Shirley, Freemantle and Bitterne Park. Economies of planning were then required; the buildings at Foundry Lane were truly 'of very plain character', with four classrooms given folding partition walls to make them 'convertible into somewhat the resemblance of a central hall.'

Headmaster of Foundry Lane Boys' School from its opening in September 1902 until retiring in March 1924 was Mr A.A. Fry – seen here at the centre of a group of his pupils. In 1910 Foundry Lane won the Schools' Football League Challenge Cup for the second successive year, winning all its fifteen matches by a total of ninety-six goals to five. Albert Fry has his own place in Saints history; he played for St Mary's YMA in its inaugural fixture on 21 November 1885, scoring two of the goals by which they defeated Freemantle five goals to one.

'Incorporation Infirmary' is the caption to this Stuart view of the forerunner of Southampton Borough/General Hospital, soon after it was built in 1900-02 by the Guardians of the Poor, i.e. the Poor Law (workhouse) authority for the six original town parishes incorporated into a Union in 1773. Extending their role from outdoor relief to public health, they bought for this hospital a site of 35 acres at Shirley Warren, which later allowed the development of a vastly expanded complex of medical facilities, following its transfer to the NHS in 1948.

This powerfully supplemented the older Royal South Hants Hospital, which made an impressive subject for Edwardian postcards; this Stuart example was used in 1906. Prompted by the disastrous High Street fire of 1837 (whose twenty-two victims are named on tablets at Holy Rood church), Drs John and William Bullar initiated raising funds to build a hospital at Newtown, opened in 1844. Financed by voluntary contributions, it was several times enlarged before coming into the NHS in 1948.

six

Monuments
and
Memorials

PALMERSTON
K.G·G.C.B.
BORN 1784
DIED 1865.
A BURGESS OF SOUTHAMPTON

ERECTED BY PUBLIC SUBSCRIPTION
FREDERICK PERKINS MAYOR
A.D. 1869

Three notable memorial statues in the central parks bearing their names were all provided by public subscriptions in the 1860s. The first to be put in hand in 1860 but not actually erected until January 1862 was for Richard Andrews (1798-1859), the poor boy who became a prosperous coachbuilder, five times Mayor of Southampton. Its fancifully ornate pedestal designed by Philip Brannon was carved in soft Bath stone which weathered badly and had to be demolished in 1971. Remounted on a plain cylinder, the statue itself (by a lesser sculptor) is now sadly unimpressive.

Isaac Watts (1674-1748), the celebrated hymn writer born and brought up in Southampton, was better-served by the 8ft statue in Sicilian marble on a pedestal representing him as a young poet, teacher and philosopher, the work of the eccentric but able sculptor Richard Cockle Lucas. Inaugurated by the Earl of Shaftesbury on 17 July 1861, it is shown above on a Stuart postcard of the early 1920s, which also features the Cenotaph, unveiled in November 1920.

The third Viscount Palmerston (1784-1865) dominated British politics for half a century as secretary for war/foreign affairs and Prime Minister. Living at Broadlands, he had various connections with Southampton, which prompted the Corporation in November 1865 to initiate subscriptions for a memorial. A well-known sculptor, Thomas Sharp, was engaged to create the statue which was eventually unveiled on 2 June 1869 – depicted here on a postcard issued around 1908 by the prolific French publisher L. Levy.

Sharp had exhibited it at the Royal Academy a year previously; his delay in delivering it to Southampton probably related to a dispute over his fee. He felt entitled to £800 but was offered only £500. His legal action in 1871 against the ex-Mayor Frederick Perkins proved inconclusive and costly, leaving Sharp aggrieved and out of pocket.

Above: Perhaps recalling the unhappy Palmerston saga, the Council was prompt in arranging its own memorial to Gen. Charles George Gordon, 'soldier, administrator, philanthropist; slain at Khartoum on 26 January, 1885'. Designed (without fee) by the borough surveyor, Mr W.B.G. Bennett, and constructed by the respected local stonemasons Messrs Garret & Haysom, this took the form of a cluster of four polished red Aberdeen granite columns, surmounted by a cross, based on a marble pedestal standing on an earth mound, to a total height of 25ft. The pedestal bore motifs and inscriptions exemplifying the general's career. Shown here on a Stuart postcard of around 1903, it was unveiled on 15 October 1885 by the mayor – who in May had opened the new Queen's Park of which it now became the centrepiece.

Right: Garret & Haysom were also responsible for the 50ft Portland stone column erected on Western Esplanade to commemorate the sailing from Southampton in 1620 of the Pilgrim Fathers aboard the *Mayflower*. The column was featured on several Stuart cards, printed in Germany, then in Britain, before and after the outbreak of war in August 1914; this example is one of the last German printings, postally used from Southampton in September 1914.

Another Garret & Haysom commission was the horse-trough placed on the Western Esplanade in 1903, 'to the loving memory of Madame Maes and the other members of the Marrett family whose house stood on this site and was built and occupied by them AD 1700-1900'. In fact dating from around 1760 and demolished in 1898, Westgate House actually straddled the old town wall, a section of which was carefully rebuilt by the borough surveyor's men in late Victorian medieval style stonework, not now distinguishable. The whole story is told in *Southampton Memorials of Care for Man and Beast*, published by the Bitterne Local History Society.

The Gas Column was erected in 1822 at the junction of Above Bar and New Road, 'by subscription as a tribute of respect and gratitude to William Chamberlyne Esq. for his munificent gifts of the iron columns supporting the public lights of the town.' Chamberlyne (who had his marine villa at Weston Grove) was Southampton MP until his death in 1829 ... and chairman of the gas lighting company. This 50ft fluted Doric column, cast at Tickell's iron foundry (recalled by Foundry Lane) was moved in 1829 to the Town Quay, where its lofty gaslight served as a 'seamark' – shown in Brannon's engraving, *c.* 1849. In 1865 the column was transferred to Houndwell, where it has twice been repositioned for traffic reasons, in 1957 and 2000.

Above: On the grass strip along the east side of The Avenue,
little noticed by motorists and pedestrians alike, stands a
distinctive piece of stonecraft, incorporating vases, scenes
of Canute rebuking his courtiers and of the sailing of
the *Mayflower.* Below the civic arms on each side of the
centre section is the inscription, 'Presented to the town
of Southampton by a native and lifelong resident in
commemoration of his 60th birthday, October 7, 1909.'
He was John Daniel Haysom, whose home was in nearby
Brighton Road, where he died only two years later. The
monument maker had created his own memorial …

A principal in the firm of Garret & Haysom (East Street
marble, granite and stone works), established in 1877 by merger
of two old family businesses, he was an active contributor to
public affairs, particularly education and heritage causes.

Right: Across the Itchen, there still stands, repositioned at the
foot of Forest Hills Drive in 1961 and refurbished in 1991, a
neat horse trough/drinking fountain (long disused as such),
originally set up at the junction of Manor Farm Road and
Woodmill Lane – as shown in this century-old photograph.
Its inscription records that it was, 'erected by a resident to
commemorate the Diamond Jubilee of Queen Victoria, June
22, 1897.' The donor was Sir Samuel Montagu MP, of South
Stoneham House, created Baron Swaythling in 1907.

A century ago, when G.D. Courtney sold his own postcards (at the chemist's shop in Derby Road he kept for thirty-five years up to 1939), their subjects included the then imposing entrance to the town cemetery. This was opened in 1846 after the Corporation had secured a special Act of Parliament in 1843 to authorise taking 15 acres of the south-west part of the common for this municipal project, made necessary by the gruesomely overcrowded state of St Mary's churchyard, where almost all the burials for the expanding town had hitherto to be made.

The Council engaged John Claudius Loudon, a well-known landscape gardener and horticultural writer who had just published a book on the layout of cemeteries, to prepare a scheme. He unfortunately died in December 1843 and his proposals were amended before work on the first 10 acres was undertaken by W.H. Rogers of Red Lodge Nurseries. The remaining 5 acres were laid out in 1863 and a further twelve were incorporated in 1884.

This cemetery, which eventually received over 116,000 burials, was superseded by another at Hollybrook, of 47 acres opened in 1913, and facilities for cremation available from 1932. After 1913 burials at the old cemetery were generally limited to use of established family plots.

Maintenance of memorials and headstones rests with holders of burial rights and descendants, now often unknown or non-existent. Despite neglect, weathering and vandalism, many thousand pieces of carved and inscribed stonework – some of them noteworthy for their artistry – still stand to memorialise people who contributed in diverse ways to the growth and development of Southampton during Victorian and Edwardian times.

Above left and right: The cemetery chapels and lodge are Grade II Listed buildings, which the City Council meets its obligation to preserve by making them available for other sympathetic uses. Taking a strictly legalistic stance, it will not, however, undertake even minimal work to maintain another similarly Listed structure … because it is a privately erected memorial.

The only one in the cemetery to be thus designated as of outstanding historical and artistic significance, this is the sculpture completed in 1864 by Richard Cockle Lucas to surmount the grave of Robert Pearce, who died aged sixty-eight in March 1861. His only son Henry Stanley Robert Pearce (1821-68) and others of the family were subsequently buried here. The Pearces were successively senior partners in the town's oldest private bank, Messrs Maddison, Pearce & Hankinson of No. 172 High Street. In 1869 this amalgamated with the other old bank, Messrs Atherley & Darwin; restyled the Union Banking Co. about 1890, this was incorporated into Lloyds Bank in 1903.

As bankers, the Pearces were doubtless respected 'worthies' of mid-Victorian Southampton so one can only speculate as to who thought of commissioning a memorial from R.C. Lucas (1800-83), a decidedly unconventional and eccentric artist. In the 1860s he was living at Chilworth, where he over-reached himself building two curiously designed houses, Chilworth Tower and the Tower of the Winds. He was saved from financial disaster by successfully applying to Lord Palmerston for a Civil List pension (£150 a year). In January 1863 he wrote, 'My public works brought me no profit … I am now getting into debt in making my master work, "The Angels of Faith, Hope, Charity bearing the Soul to Paradise."'

Erected in September 1864, this was much admired, described by the *Southampton Times* as comprising, 'three life sized winged figures of Faith, Hope and Charity supporting a mortuary urn with a butterfly emerging from the chrysalis state emblematic of human resurrection … on the figures which represent the cardinal attributes of the Christian character the artist has lavished the highest order of poetic conception and manipulative skills.'

Above left and right: This monument (right) to Joseph Rankin Stebbing, who died in 1874 aged sixty-four, was, 'erected by the members of Southampton Chamber of Commerce of which he was for many years president'. That this inscription can be read is due to the civic-minded volunteers of the Friends of Southampton Old Cemetery who, in 2005, cleared the overgrowth which had made it look like a tree (left). The City Council's management of the cemetery 'is now timed to benefit nature. This does not conflict with the historical importance of the site which provides an insight into the social history of the City and its maritime roots.' A balance is not easy to strike; other roots render significant memorials overgrown and unsightly. FoSOC members now devote time and labour to clearing and caring for some of them.

Opposite left: J.R. Stebbing, portrayed here from an anonymous painting in Southampton Art Gallery, made important contributions to the town's public affairs through four decades, as a zealous promoter of its commercial and port interests and advocate of improved provision for public health, adult education etc. Coming from Portsmouth in 1831, he set up a High Street business as optician and mathematical and nautical instrument maker, also ships' chandler. He was elected a councillor in 1838, alderman in 1865 and mayor in 1867. He was respected for his foresight, energy, eloquence and tolerance, always seeking consensus for progress. In January 1851 he was the prime mover in establishing the Chamber of Commerce, one of the country's earliest. He was its first president and held office again from 1855 to 1866.

Above right: Until cleared by FoSOC volunteers yearly in 2006, thick brambles engulfed the draped urn and boulder memorial to Francis Godolphin Osborne Stuart, the celebrated postcard-publishing photographer, and 'his dearly beloved wife Agnes Isabella', who died in 1923 and 1900 respectively.

Besides such projects, the Friends of Southampton Old Cemetery provide an extensive programme of expertly conducted cemetery walks on a range of themes, publish leaflets and newsletters and offer services of family grave location and care.

Below: Close to 'Faith, Hope and Charity' is another noteworthy memorial. Its conventional weather-beaten stonework of 1850 is surmounted by a carving not now immediately identifiable as an upturned lifeboat, specially designed to fit over the paddle wheel boxes of early steamships. Once widely acclaimed but long since superseded, this was one of the several inventions of George Smith, a naval officer who served afloat from 1808 until appointed commander in charge of gunnery instructions at HMS *Excellent*, Portsmouth, in 1830. There he made significant contributions to this aspect of naval warfare and other maritime developments. In 1849 he was transferred to Southampton, as superintendent of Royal Mail Packets; he died the following year, still in his early sixties.

A neatly carved relief portrait adorns this headstone erected 'in loving memory of Louisa Fanny Algeo, daughter of Captain Robert Moresby and wife of Colonel Horace Albert Brown, Commissioner of Pegu, British Burma, who died at sea off Madras on the 24th July 1880 and whose remains were interred here on the 17th August'. They were buried in front of the memorial to her parents, Captain Robert Moresby of the Indian Navy, who died in 1851, and 'Mary his beloved wife'.

The cemetery contains many other reminders of bygone imperial times when military and naval men – often accompanied by their dedicated wives – spent much of their lives abroad serving the British Raj and Empire.

Below: This memorial to Josiah George Poole (1818–97) looks pristine because it was photographed for Garret & Haysom soon after it was put on his grave. Recent clearance of earth and vegetation has revealed the name of the man who left his mark on the town which he served as architect, surveyor and valuer.

From 1848 he was successively surveyor to the Improvement Commissioners, Local Board of Health and Borough Council. For the latter he was responsible for the painstakingly authentic restoration of the south side of the Bargate in 1864–65; earlier he pioneered the use of glued laminate timber arches in an 1860 schoolroom for King Edward VI School – now the marriage room of the registry office in Bugle Street. Leaving the Corporation in 1866 (when he was succeeded by James Lemon), he continued to work for the South Hants Building Society and in private practice. His other works included the first sewerage scheme for Shirley in 1866–68. From 1871 J.G. Poole was surveyor to the Harbour Board, assisted by his son Edward Cooper-Poole, who took over in 1887 and served until his death in 1935.

In the 1850s and again in the 1880s he leased Old Palace House, No. 9 St Michael's Square, the central part of Tudor House Museum, where he lived with some of his large family – twenty-one children from his two marriages.

On his memorial Andrew Lamb (1803–81) is identified as, 'for well-nigh forty years the first Superintendent of the Peninsular and Oriental Steam Navigation Company'. A Scot, he came to the town in 1841 to serve the company until it transferred its headquarters to London in 1875. Lamb did much to raise the status of ships' engineers and made important innovations in marine engineering. In the 1840s he bought part of the old Bellevue estate to build himself a villa and donate the site for St Andrew's Presbyterian church, with which he was closely associated. (Opened in 1853, it was demolished in 1995.) Besides being much involved with various charitable activities, Lamb was the first chairman of the Southampton & Isle of Wight Steam Packet Co. (Red Funnel) from 1861 and was for many years a busy alderman and JP.

His only son, Andrew Simon Lamb, whose memorial stands to the right of his father's, became a barrister and, likewise, devoted himself to religious and philanthropic causes.

The monument to Sir James Lemon (1833–1923) describes him as, 'much esteemed for his many interests and for his activities in connection with the town'. The many-sided career of this notable civil engineer is outlined in *Southampton, The Second Selection*, page 47.

This emblematic headstone near the Hill Lane entrance to the Old Cemetery is, 'Sacred to the memory of Lt-Gen Sir Henry James, Director of the Ordnance Survey from 1855 to 1875'. Born in 1803, Sir Henry James was commissioned into the Royal Engineers in 1826 and was soon posted to the OS, with which he served all his career, apart from an interlude as chief engineer in Portsmouth dockyard. He actually took up his Southampton appointment in 1854, as stated on the 'blue plaque' recently erected at his official residence, Avenue House, on the corner of Rockstone Place and The Avenue.

He vigorously tackled OS problems of delayed production, mapping scales, photographic printing and scientific investigations, earning a knighthood in 1860. Failing health caused him to retire in 1875; he died in 1877.

Below: A plaque erected over the doorway of No. 21 Carlton Crescent during the Southampton meeting of the British Association in 1925 records that, 'in this house from 1861 to 1881 lived Col. A.R. Clarke CB, FRS, who determined the figure of the earth'. Alexander Ross Clarke (1828–1914) passed out top of his year at Woolwich and joined the Royal Engineers; a posting to the OS gave full scope for his mathematical talents. He also made time for a full family life, his marriage being blessed with four sons and nine daughters.

He organised publication of masses of survey data, including an international project to calculate the exact dimensions of the earth, and wrote a standard book on geodesy (1880). Col. Clarke was elected a

Fellow of the Royal Society in 1862 and was honoured by other learned societies, but in 1881 someone at the War Office decided that after twenty-seven years in Southampton he should be posted overseas. He objected, and when protests from scientific circles went unheeded, he resigned and went into retirement in Surrey.

'Presented to the town of Southampton by the Institution of Mechanical Engineers in 1955', a plaque on the medieval West Gate records that, 'in a cellar near this place' Walter Taylor and his son of the same name, 'developed inventions of great importance to the Royal Navy between the years 1750 and 1758'.

Other commemorative plaques erected under various auspices range widely in their subjects, from one at No. 5 Rockstone Place noting that, 'In this house lived the hero of Khartoum, General Charles George Gordon, Chinese Gordon B. 1833, D. 1885', to the tablet identifying No. 11 Portland Street as, 'from 1866 to 1892 the home of Mathilde, Alice and Adela Verne, who achieved great distinction and world fame as pianists, teachers of the pianoforte and composers'. Born in 1865, 1868 and 1877 respectively, they were the talented daughters of John Evangelist Wurm and his wife Sophie who

came from Bavaria to settle in Southampton around 1860; both were music teachers. Following their father's death, the sisters adopted the anglicised name of Verne in 1893.

At the Above Bar end of Portland Street is a plaque stating, 'John Everett Millais, 1829-1896, Pre-Raphaelite painter and President of the Royal Academy, was born in a house near this spot', erected by the City Council in 1996 to mark the centenary of his death. This was most probably the one formerly occupied by Gilbert's bookshop but the Council was taking care not to repeat its error of 1994, when a plaque naming it as the birthplace of Emily Davies (1830-1921), 'campaigner for Women's Education', was placed on the wrong house in Carlton Crescent. It was subsequently removed and in 2004 an English Heritage blue plaque was correctly positioned on No. 6 Carlton Crescent.

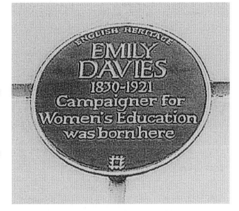

In addition to Sir Henry James, others similarly commemorated that year were: No. 38 Chessel Avenue – 'Roy Chadwick 1893-1947, Designer of the Lancaster and Vulcan bomber aircraft, lived here 1922-1929'; No. 38 Brookvale Road – 'Herbert Collins 1885-1975, Architect of Suburbia, lived here 1930-1973'; No. 1 Cranbury Place – 'John Jellicoe, First Earl Jellicoe 1859-1935, Admiral of the Fleet, was born here.'

In September 2005 a sixth blue plaque was unveiled at No. 2 Russell Place, stating, 'R.J. Mitchell 1895-1937, Designer of the Supermarine Spitfire lived here 1927-1937.'

Mr J.V. Candy, formerly the 57th Sheriff and 764th Mayor of the City and prominent member of the City of Southampton Society, has compiled a comprehensive list entitled *Heritage: People, Plaques and Places in Southampton.*

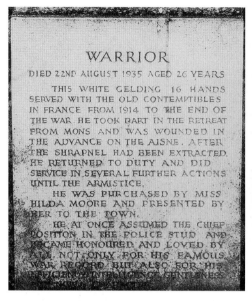

WARRIOR

DIED 22ND AUGUST 1935 AGED 26 YEARS

THIS WHITE GELDING 16 HANDS
SERVED WITH THE OLD CONTEMPTIBLES
IN FRANCE FROM 1914 TO THE END OF
THE WAR. HE TOOK PART IN THE RETREAT
FROM MONS AND WAS WOUNDED IN
THE ADVANCE ON THE AISNE. AFTER
THE SHRAPNEL HAD BEEN EXTRACTED
HE RETURNED TO DUTY AND DID
SERVICE IN SEVERAL FURTHER ACTIONS
UNTIL THE ARMISTICE.
HE WAS PURCHASED BY MISS
HILDA MOORE AND PRESENTED BY
HER TO THE TOWN.
HE AT ONCE ASSUMED THE CHIEF
POSITION IN THE POLICE STUD AND
BECAME HONOURED AND LOVED BY
ALL NOT ONLY FOR HIS FAMOUS
WAR RECORD BUT ALSO FOR HIS
EFFICIENCY INTELLIGENCE GENTLENESS

Above left and right: At the Sports Centre, by the golf course, stands an unusual gravestone, erected in 1935 at the instance of the Council leader, Alderman Sir Sidney Kimber. Headed, 'Warrior, died 22 August 1934, aged 26 years', it carries this almost lyrical inscription:

This white gelding, 16 hands, served with the 'Old Contemptibles' in France from 1914 to the end of the War. He took part in the retreat from Mons and was wounded in the advance on the Aisne. After the shrapnel had been extracted he returned to duty and did service in several further actions until the Armistice. He was purchased by Miss Hilda Moore and presented by her to the Town. He at once assumed the chief position in the Police Stud and became honoured and loved by all, not only for his famous war record but also for his efficiency, intelligence, gentleness and noble character.

This notable animal was given his name by Miss Hilda Moore, of the Glen, Banister Park, the horse-loving lady who initiated his purchase from Army surplus stables and gave him to the borough police authority in May 1919 – stipulating that he should be brought to her house for an annual 'birthday present' of sugar.

Whatever the role of a gelding as head of the Police Stud, Warrior was prominent among the mounted section that between the wars patrolled the common and outlying parts of the town as well as heading parades and processions, particularly of ex-servicemen.

Three of Warrior's hooves were formed into inkstands, presented to the mayor; the other one became a gavel for use at meetings of the Old Contemptibles Association local branch.

seven

Disasters, Victims and Heroes

From the 1840s a mainstay of port development at Southampton was the Royal Mail Steam Packet Co. running mail contract and passenger services to the West Indies and South America.

In the early years its steamers were sadly accident-prone. On the wall of the south aisle of St Michael's church is a tablet erected by the company, 'in honour of the captain, officers and crew who perished in the destruction of the *Amazon* steam-ship by fire on 4th January 1852'. Only two days out of port on her maiden voyage, this Thames-built 2,256-ton paddle steamer caught fire when her engines overheated; she sank within a few hours, claiming the lives of 105 of the 164 aboard.

The *Amazon* had been acclaimed 'the largest timber-built ship ever constructed in England'. Because they were classed as reserve frigates, the Admiralty insisted mail steamers were built of wood, rather than iron, which it feared would shatter under gunfire. After the 1852 disaster, it allowed Royal Mail ships to be built of iron, which reduced fire risks but could not save them from the ferocity of Caribbean hurricanes – as cruelly demonstrated in 1867.

In the Old Cemetery is a prominent tall monument, 'in memory of the officers and crew of the Royal Mail Steamships *Rhone* and *Wye* lost during the hurricane at St Thomas, West Indies, October 29, 1867'. The *Rhone*, 2,738 tons, built at Millwall only two years earlier, was there (in the Virgin Islands, then Danish, acquired by the United States in 1917) preparing to return to Southampton when she was caught by the fierce winds and blown on to rocks where she broke in two and sank. Only twenty-one of her 129 crew and one of her sixteen passengers survived.

The *Wye*, a smaller vessel of 819 tons, built in 1853, suffered a similar fate, losing forty-one of her sixty-nine crew. Altogether, that 1867 hurricane damaged or destroyed over sixty ships and claimed about 1,000 lives.

The sister ship of the *Rhone* was the *Douro*, which survived the hurricane and brought the first full account of that disaster back to Southampton in November 1867. Fifteen years later, she was sunk at sea, as recalled by another memorial nearby.

Its square base, topped by a pink granite column bearing a cross and anchor, is inscribed, 'to the memory of Captain E.C. Kemp, the officers, engineers and crew of the … ship *Douro*, who perished at sea on 1st April, 1882, nobly sacrificing their lives that others might be saved'. This is flanked by other lettering noting, 'foundered after collision' and 'this monument is erected by their brother officers and friends'. A panel lists fifteen names – arranged in order of rank.

A popular ship on the South American service, the *Douro* was heading home from Lisbon, some 35 miles north of Cape Finisterre, on a clear night, when she was inexplicably struck amidships by the 2,197-ton Spanish steamer *Yrurac Bat*. The impact damage was such that both ships sank within half an hour. Of the sixty-six people aboard the latter, thirty-six were lost but most of the *Douro* boats were safely launched, to save all but six of her sixty passengers. A fifth of the crew of seventy-five gave their lives, devoting themselves to the care of passengers. Fortunately, the steamer *Hidalgo* was near enough to pick up 144 survivors within a few hours.

This maritime disaster was greatly felt in Southampton, where many of the Royal Mail crews lived. As for the *Rhone* and *Wye* catastrophe, the mayor opened a relief fund to aid bereaved families.

Saint-Malo — Naufrage du " HILDA " (19 novembre 1905)
L'arrière du navire et le pont brisé

Above and below: Among several further mayoral relief funds to aid the families of victims of maritime disasters involving Southampton-based ships was that occasioned by the wreck of the LSWR steamer *Hilda*, caught in a blinding snowstorm and driven on to the rocks outside St Malo on the night of the 18/19 November, 1905.

Her loss had an impact on Southampton comparable to that of the *Titanic* in 1912. Although much smaller in scale, the disaster was no less sudden and unexpected, with proportionately greater casualties. Only one of her twenty-eight crew (all local men) and five of her 105 passengers survived; in the twenty-seven families of her lost crewmen, there were eighteen widows, with fifty children left fatherless.

The *Hilda* was an iron screw steamer of 848 tons; Glasgow-built in 1882, she had made hundreds of uneventful crossings on the Southampton – St Malo service. Dashed on sharp rocks and broken in two, her wreckage was soon photographed for enterprising St Malo publishers for a series of topical postcards. Their subjects included a close-up of the midships section and wheelhouse and a view of French divers seeking to recover bodies.

Saint-Malo — Naufrage du " HILDA " (Nuit du 18 au 19 novembre 1905)
Scaphandriers recherchant les cadavres

Right: Capt. William Gregory (1849-1905) joined the LSWR service in 1869 and from 1880 became master of several cross-channel steamers before taking command of the *Hilda* in 1895. Well qualified, skilled and experienced, he was respected both professionally and for his genial personality. He made his home at No. 78 Tennyson Road, Portswood.

Inquest and Inquiry hearings found that after the *Hilda* was swept into a cleft in the rocks, making it impossible to launch her boats, captain and crew did all they could in the circumstances; no-one could be blamed for the loss of the *Hilda*. Before the advent of radio and radar, such events were sadly frequent. After bodies were recovered, Gregory's was the first of twelve to be buried in the Old Cemetery; others were interred at churchyards east of the Itchen.

Below: The *Hilda* carried 105 passengers – twenty-five British and eighty French, the latter being Breton onion sellers returning home after their annual trading visits. Only five Bretons survived; along with AB James Grinter, they managed to cling to the rigging throughout the night, while the chief mate and others froze and dropped off to their deaths. They probably owed their lives to the masthead lamp remaining alight, to shed a little warmth on those nearest it. After twelve agonising hours, they were seen next morning and rescued by boat from the *Hilda*'s sister ship *Ada* leaving St Malo.

James Grinter was a sturdy man, then in his fifties, living with his large family in Newtown. Recovering from his ordeal, he grave graphic accounts of his experiences – and obliged well-wishers by autographing postcards like the one below. Understandably, he never returned to sea but found a Customs job in the docks. He lived on into his eighties, dying in 1935.

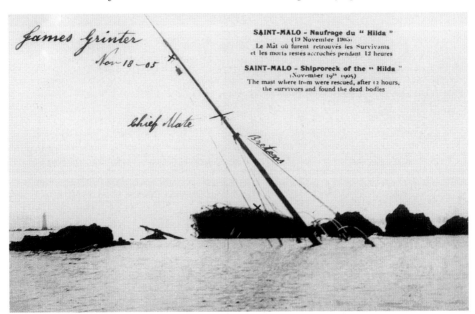

SAINT-MALO - Naufrage du " Hilda "
(19 Novembre 1905)
Le Mât où furent retrouvés les Survivants
et les morts restes accrochés pendant 12 heures

SAINT-MALO - Shipwreck of the " Hilda "
(November 19th 1905)
The mast where from were rescued, after 12 hours,
the survivors and found the dead bodies

Above: One of the stewardesses lost in the *Hilda* tragedy was Mrs Mary Ann Hubbard, whose husband had drowned in the wreck of another LSWR steamer, the *Stella* (1059 tons, Clyde-built in 1890). The heroine of that disaster was another widow, Mrs Mary Ann Rogers, who likewise worked for the LSWR after her husband had died in the company's service. As senior stewardess of the *Stella*, which struck rocks near Alderney on 30 March 1899 causing the deaths of nearly half the 200 people aboard, Mrs Rogers sacrificed her life to help save passengers in her care. The full story is told in *Southampton Memorials of Care for Man and Beast*. Ladies 'kindly tended' by Mrs Rogers on previous passages to the Channel Islands raised a public subscription to help her aged father and orphaned children and erect a memorial to her heroism. A neat canopied structure of Portland stone sited on the Western Esplanade, this was photographed soon after its unveiling on 27 July 1901, for a popular Stuart postcard.

Above: In the early 1900s, when newspapers carried few illustrations, photographers like F.G.O. Stuart found a ready market for postcards depicting topical events, particularly maritime disasters.

'Raising the S.Y. EROS by the Western Marine Salvage Co. in Southampton Water, Sept. 22nd 1907', was the caption to this Stuart card, quickly produced in black and white by his British printer. Its subject was the 770-ton luxury steam yacht, built on the Thames in 1885 for Baron de Rothschild. She was acquired early in 1907 by Robert Houston, a Liverpool ship owner and MP.

He did not long enjoy his ownership, for on the night of 3 September, while lying at anchor some 500 yards from the head of Hythe Pier, the *Eros* was run into by a Liverpool collier, the 2,635-ton *Knightsgarth*, outward bound from Southampton. Her bow penetrated halfway through the yacht's framework and when the collier was taken astern, the *Eros* sank almost immediately, settling in the mud in about 15ft of water. Happily, there was time for all aboard her to be rescued by boats from other nearby yachts and the *Knightsgarth*. The cause of the collision remained a mystery, for her skipper was a reliable and experienced man, the night was calm and both vessels had lights.

The recovery of the *Eros* was entrusted by Lloyds to a Penzance firm, which patched her holes and pumped her afloat on 22 September; she was towed to No. 1 Dry Dock, where Thornycrofts repaired her. In May 1908 she was sold to the British agent for the West African republic of Liberia, for use as a gunboat on coastal patrol duties. After alterations by Summers & Payne in the Inner Dock and being fitted with guns at Portsmouth, she received a civic send-off on 5 October when she sailed from Southampton under command of a seconded British naval officer. The *Eros* was renamed RLS *Lark*, reviving the name of Liberia's first 'navy', a small armed vessel lent by the Admiralty in 1849. The second *Lark* did useful service until disused, *c.* 1925.

Opposite below: This gravestone in the Old Cemetery is unusual for being inscribed in both English and German. Clearance by FoSOC members enables one to read that it was erected by the crew of the SS *Philadelphia* and the Seamen's Union of Hoboken, New Jersey, in loving memory of Hermann Schultz and Franz Frzewik, aged thirty-one and forty-one respectively, accidentally killed in Southampton Docks on 12 July 1903. They were firemen on the *Philadelphia*, a 10,500-ton vessel built in 1889, originally named *City of Paris*, acquired in 1893 by the American Line, which that year moved the terminus of its New York service from Liverpool to Southampton. The deaths of Schultz and Frzewik were sudden and unexpected; making their way back to their ship in the Empress Dock late at night they were run over by a shunting goods train and killed instantly.

Above and below: Other Stuart cards of 1907 recall a remarkable salvage and reconstruction achievement involving the *Suevic*, a 12,500-ton liner built in 1901 by Harland & Wolff at Belfast for White Star services to Australia. On the night of 17 March 1907 a navigational error in foggy weather drove her hard on the rocks near the Lizard. Local lifeboats and tugs took off all 456 persons aboard; most of her cargo was later removed but the vessel could not be refloated. Capt. Fred Young, in charge of salvage, organised cutting the ship in two by ingenious controlled dynamiting. In April the stern section was towed to Southampton, partly under its own steam. A new bow unit was then built at Belfast and – as shown on a topical postcard, below – towed in October to Southampton, where it was skilfully joined to the repaired stern section.

   The *Suevic* resumed service in January 1908, continuing until 1928, when she was sold to Norway, to become the whale factory ship *Skytteren*. In 1942 she was scuttled by her crew to prevent capture by German warships while trying to escape to Britain.

Above: In an unseasonably fierce snowstorm and blinding blizzard on the afternoon of 25 April 1908 the American Line's *St Paul*, which had just left Southampton for New York, ran into the 5,750-ton cruiser *HMS Gladiator*, striking her amidships and sinking her with loss of twenty-eight of her ship's company. The 11,629-ton liner was able to return to Southampton, for Harland & Wolff to repair her damaged bow in the Trafalgar dry dock, where G.D. Courtney was soon on the scene to photograph her for topical postcards. Passengers from the *St Paul*, unharmed, left aboard the *Teutonic* on 29 April. The *St Paul* resumed services on 20 June.

Below: F.G.O. Stuart issued cards showing the *Gladiator* lying on her deeply gashed starboard side in low water near Yarmouth pier. Lightening, patching, balancing and refloating her, directed by Capt. F.W. Young of the Liverpool Salvage Association, proved a difficult operation, taking five months before she could be righted and towed to Portsmouth. The wreck was sold to a ship breaker for less than a third of the £50,000 paid by the Admiralty for salvage work.

Another liner-cruiser collision in the Solent, fortunately free of casualties, occurred on 20 September 1911; in daylight and on a calm sea, the 7,300-ton HMS *Hawke* sliced into the *Olympic*. Then briefly the world's largest, at 45,324 tons, she was newly built by Harland & Wolff for the White Star Line, which had transferred its transatlantic services from Liverpool in 1907, enhancing Southampton's status as a major passenger port.

The cruiser's bow tore a 40ft-long gash in the liner's starboard side near the stern, as shown on this postcard issued by the local marine photographer Adolphe Rapp of Bernard Street. The *Hawke* was taken to Portsmouth for dry dock repairs, while the *Olympic* limped back to Southampton and then to Belfast for repairs lasting six months. She later underwent safety refitting there, then served as a troopship in the First World War and continued New York – Southampton service until withdrawn in 1935 for scrapping.

The sister ships of the *Olympic* were sadly short-lived. The tragedy of the *Titanic* – shown here leaving Southampton on her ill-fated maiden voyage on 10 April 1912 – is all too well known. Ironically, that voyage might have been delayed had she not narrowly missed colliding with the smaller liner *New York*, which the *Titanic*'s powerful suction tore from her mooring stern-first. The collision between the *Olympic* and HMS *Hawke* was attributed to the liner's suction acting on the cruiser.

'Huntspill sunk in Southampton Docks, Feb. 27, 1921' is the caption to this topical postcard produced by John Jarvis from his Express Studio at No. 21 Canal Walk – convenient to the docks for him to hasten there on a Sunday morning to record the unusual scene of a 5,440-ton troopship lying on a mud bank beside Berth 41.

Contrasting with the maritime disasters previously recounted, the sinking of the *Huntspill* at her quayside mooring was trivial, even risible. It was an embarrassment to her owners, the Ministry of Shipping, which doubtless discouraged further sightseers and press attention to an event which must have attracted much interest at the time. The story merits retelling. Originally named *Koerber*, the *Huntspill* was a passenger steamer built at Trieste by and for the Lloyd Austriaco Co. From 1904 she ran services to Africa and the Far East, until taken at Port Said in August 1914 as a British war prize. Put to duty as a troopship in the Mediterranean, she became one of a score of ex-enemy ships given new names beginning with 'Hun'. In 1920-21 the *Huntspill* was fitted up at Southampton to carry garrison troops to and from India. On Saturday evening, 26 February 1921, three days before she was due to sail, her ballast tanks were being emptied and cleaned out for fresh water to be pumped in. A Court of Inquiry later found that 'she had a list of rather more than one and a half degrees', which increased until, within ten minutes, an inrush of water flooded the vessel, causing her to heel over, part her moorings and sink, to lie on her port side at an angle of about fifteen degrees.

The Court heard that most of the inflow came through the aperture left by removal for repair of the ash ejector chest valve and a light on the port side, added to which many of the port lights had been left open to air and dry the troop quarters on the orlop deck. Charitably, the Inquiry did not attribute the founding of the *Huntspill* to 'any wrongful act or default by her Master and officers' – who were all ashore at the time.

The sunken vessel was later raised and salvaged, to be returned in September to the Italian successor to her original owner-operator. Renamed *Asia*, she resumed services to that continent, until withdrawn in 1933 for breaking up.

Capt. Charles Fryatt, portrayed here on a 1919 Belgian postcard with his ship, the SS *Brussels*, was, as its caption says, 'captured by the Germans on 23 June, 1916 and shot at Bruges on 27 July 1916'. Acclaimed as a hero and martyr of the First World War, he was born at No. 6 Marsh Lane, Southampton, on 2 December 1871, son of a merchant seaman. He first attended Holy Trinity National School, then transferred to Freemantle Boys' School in March 1882 after his family had moved to that suburb. Charles left in October 1883, to finish his education at Harwich, where his father went to join the steamer service of the Great Eastern Railway. Son followed father afloat, working his way up to become a ship's master by 1913.

In the First World War (when Holland remained neutral) Capt. Fryatt became the best known of the 'pirate dodgers' running the gauntlet of enemy attacks from bases in Belgium. He was credited with making 143 such trips. His first notable encounter with a German submarine was on 2 March 1915, when the SS *Wrexham* evaded her pursuer over a 40-mile chase to Rotterdam. On 28 March, now commanding the *Brussels*, he steamed full speed at the U33, firing off rockets to give the impression of guns, to force it to submerge by threat of ramming. These exploits were highly commended in Britain, with gold watches awarded him by both the GER and the Admiralty.

While the British authorities considered merchant vessels fully entitled to resist capture or sinking, the Germans took a different view of such 'civilian' defiance. Publicity of Capt. Fryatt's exploits made him a marked man in their eyes and sealed his fate when the *Brussels* was captured by German destroyers on 23 June 1916. He was court martialled at Bruges, quickly convicted of being a *franc tireur*, not part of a regular armed force, sentenced to death and shot within an hour. His execution proved a political misjudgement, arousing widespread condemnation as a 'judicial murder'.

In July 1919 Charles Fryatt's body was exhumed, returned to England and drawn on a gun carriage to St Paul's Cathedral for a national memorial service, then taken by special train for burial with full military honours at Dovercourt, where he had lived. His memory was honoured in Belgium, with which he had a connection only in his captivity and death. He remains a national hero there; the ninetieth anniversary of his execution was marked by a commemorative exhibition and other tributes – in which representatives of Freemantle School were involved.

The remains of an old wooden propeller make an unusual adjunct to the Moon family monument in the Old Cemetery. It carries a plaque, 'in affectionate memory of Squadron Leader E.R. Moon, DSO, RAF, killed on 29 April 1920 in the service of his country: erected by his comrades of No. 230 Squadron Royal Air Force Felixstowe'. This is thought to come from the aircraft in which he commanded a training flight that day. The inquest verdict was 'death from injuries received through the sudden accidental fall of a flying boat.'

Born in 1886, educated at Banister Court and Cranleigh Schools, Edwin Rowland Moon developed engineering skills which he applied to construct two experimental monoplanes, making some short local flights in 1910. His workshop was in the old Wool House, where he became manager of Moonbeams Ltd, the business started by his uncle Egbert to market marine engines and motor launches. On the outbreak of war, Moon joined the RNAS, obtaining his aviator's certificate in October 1914 – from which this photograph is taken. Following coastal sorties from Felixstowe, he was posted in 1916 to undertake ship-based flying boat operations against German East Africa. Engine failure and forced landing led to him spending 1917 as a POW. Repatriated, his exploits recognised by the DSO and bar, he afterwards became commander of the flying boat station at Felixstowe.

The only Southampton man awarded the Victoria Cross in 1914–18 was Lt Cdr Daniel Marcus William Beak (1891–1967). An old boy of Taunton's School, he joined the RNVR on the outbreak of war and gave distinguished service in France, becoming commander of the Drake Battalion of the Naval Brigade. Having already won the MC and DSO, he received the VC in August 1918, 'for his conspicuous bravery, courageous leadership and devotion to duty during a prolonged period of operations'. He made his career in the army and served with the Eighth Army in North Africa before retiring in 1945 with the rank of Major General.

The sole Southampton recipient of a VC in the Second World War was also an Old Tauntonian. Jack Foreman Mantle, born in London on 12 April 1917, came with his family around 1922 to Southampton, where his father Walter joined the Borough Engineer's staff. Jack attended Western District and Taunton's Schools, leaving the latter in 1931 to work for a year on a New Forest farm before entering the Royal Navy in May 1933 as a boy of sixteen. He saw service on the China and Mediterranean stations and had become a Leading Seaman by 1940, when he was established as a gunner on HMS *Foylebank*. This was one of three cruisers attacked and sunk in Portland Harbour by a score of German dive bombers on 4 July 1940. His gallantry that day is recounted in the official citation for the VC, posthumously awarded, which his parents received from King George VI at Buckingham Palace on 24 June 1941:

> Leading Seaman Jack Mantle was in charge of the starboard pom-pom when the Foylebank was attacked by enemy aircraft. Early in the action his left leg was shattered by a bomb but he stood fast at his gun and went on firing with the hand-gear only, for the ship's electric power had failed. Almost at once he was wounded again in many places. Between his bursts of fire he had time to reflect on the grievous injuries of which he was soon to die; but his great courage bore him up till the end of the fight, when he fell by the gun he had so valiantly served.

A plaque bearing this citation was erected in 1950 at the 'Jack's Corner' memorial playground at the Sports Centre; in 1985 it was transferred to the Maritime Museum.

Leading Seaman Jack Mantle is here pictured from an informal family photograph, courtesy his sister, Mrs B Corlett.

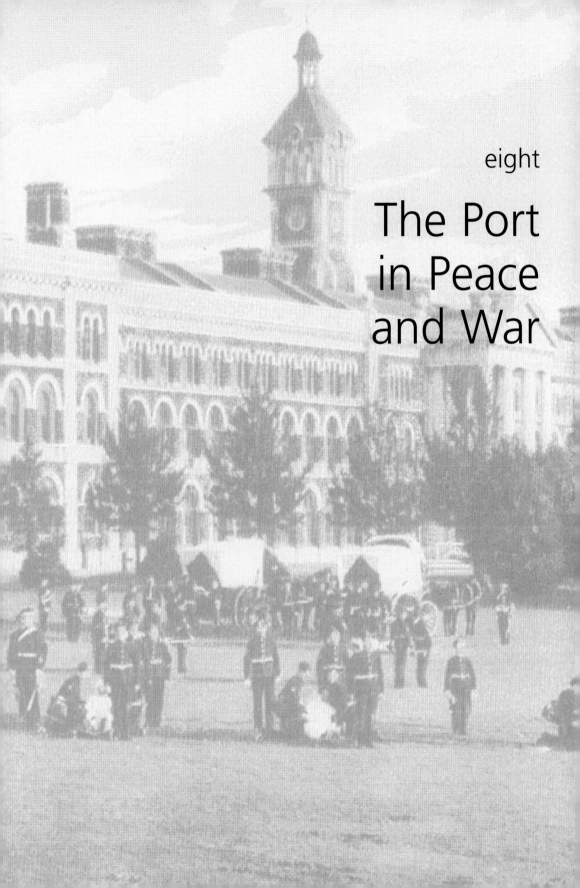

eight

The Port
in Peace
and War

Above: Southampton was not a naval port but its maritime status was recognised by the Admiralty bestowing its name on a succession of warships, beginning with a forty-eight-gun 'wooden wall' built at Chapel in 1693. The third HMS *Southampton*, a sixty-gun heavy frigate launched at Deptford in 1820, saw world-wide service before becoming a training ship in 1868. Moored off Victoria Pier, Kingston-upon-Hull, this accommodated up to 250 homeless and destitute boys aged eleven to sixteen, until the school closed in 1912 and the old vessel was sold to breakers. She is here pictured from a postcard, *c.* 1905.

Below: Her successor, Clyde-built in 1912, was a Chatham class 5,400-ton light cruiser. Part of the Grand Fleet in 1914-18, she survived a fierce engagement in the Battle of Jutland and, after repairs, continued in service until sold for breaking up in 1926. HMS *Southampton* is here depicted in 1918, 'dazzle' painted to break up her silhouette and confuse would-be attackers as to her actual location and course.

The fifth HMS *Southampton* was launched on the Clyde in 1936, the 9,600-ton nameship of a new class of cruisers. She was lost in 1941 after being bombed and set on fire by German planes off Sicily. The present, sixth, bearer of the city's name is a 3,800-ton guided missile destroyer, built by Thornycroft at Woolston in 1979.

Above and below: Two spirited engravings by Philip Brannon evoke busy scenes around the pier and docks about 1850 – the product of an exciting decade of development that saw the completion of the LSWR line to London and the construction from 1842 onwards of a series of docks. Catering for the ocean-going steamships, these promoted the further growth of the port previously fostered by the building of the pier in 1833 to provide landing stages for the early paddle steamer services.

The Peninsular and Oriental Co. made Southampton its base in 1840, soon followed by the Royal Mail Steam Packet Co.; in the 1850s the Union Steamship Co. (and later the Castle Line with which it merged in 1899) became the third mainstay of the port's passenger and mail contract trade. German and other foreign vessels also began calling at Southampton from 1857 onwards.

Southampton, Trafalgar Graving Dock. Largest Dry Dock in the World. 8061

As more and larger liners came to Southampton, the Docks Company extended its facilities but found demand exceeding its resources – a situation highlighted by the P & O Company transferring its operations to London in 1881. The LSWR helped finance the Empress Dock, opened by Queen Victoria on 26 July 1890, and in 1892 took over the Docks Company It proceeded to construct two new dry docks, named Prince of Wales (opened in 1895) and Trafalgar – appropriately opened on 21 October 1905. Measuring 912ft x 100ft, this was acclaimed 'the largest dry dock in the world' in the caption to this contemporary postcard.

One of Stuart's earliest postcards reproduced this photograph taken in August/September 1889. It shows the new 6,660-ton P & O steamer *Arcadia* on her only visit to Southampton, as one of several vessels diverted there during the great dock strike which closed the port of London for several weeks. This Stuart card went through numerous editions from 1902 into the 1920s, when the port was handling liners nearly ten times bigger than the *Arcadia*.

Above and below: With its unique double tides and strategic location, Southampton was well-placed to become Britain's 'Gateway to the World' but it needed another large dock to cater for liners of 40,000 tons or more. Construction work in 1909-11 attracted great interest, not least from photographers who provided topical pictures for several postcard publishers.

Providing another 3,800 feet of quay, this 15-acre project was originally styled the White Star Dock, being primarily related to the liners of that company, which had transferred the terminal of its transatlantic services from Liverpool in 1907. In 1922, after Cunard and Canadian Pacific had likewise moved their operations to Southampton, it was renamed Ocean Dock.

From 1840 shipbuilding on the Itchen was centred at the Northam Iron Works, where Day, Summers & Co. produced steamships including two of 3,000 tons in 1869 – The *Hindostan* (P & O) and the *Nile* (Royal Mail). Their builders later specialised in engineering services e.g. patent sheerlegs and slipways, but also constructed tugs, ferries and luxury steam yachts. The business closed in 1929, when most of the site was taken over by Thornycrofts. J.I. Thornycroft & Co. Ltd had moved their operations in 1904 from Chiswick to Woolston, where an extensive shipyard had passed through three short-lived ownerships following the departure in 1889 of Thomas Ridley Oswald, who had created it from 1875.

Born in 1836, Oswald had worked at his uncle's Sunderland yard before setting up on his own at twenty-one. In 1875, having already produced 150 ships, mostly in iron, his quest for a new location brought him to Woolston, along with many of his workforce from Wearside. In 1878 he took into partnership John Murray Mordaunt, a Warwickshire gentleman who provided capital for expansion. Oswald, Mordaunt & Co. were soon employing 1,000 men at peak periods. In thirteen years from 1876, 104 ships were launched at Woolston; a third were steamships (the largest, 5,085 tons, built in 1883, was briefly named *Bitterne)* but the majority were sturdy three-masted full-rigged sailing ships of around 2,000 tons. Distinctively styled, capable of passages comparable to a clipper, they reflected the input of Hercules Linton, designer of the *Cutty Sark*, who worked for Oswald in the 1880s.

Mostly built for Liverpool companies, they served worldwide as long-haul carriers of coal, lumber, grain, nitrates etc. in the period when sail was still cheaper than steam for such bulk cargoes. Many of Oswald's ships were remarkably long-lived. Pictured above, the *Wavertree* is the oldest and most celebrated, a 2,150-ton vessel launched on 10 December 1885. From 1888 she ran cargo voyages around the world for the Leyland company of Liverpool until 1910 when she was sold to Ernest Neal. He got a coal cargo to Chile but the *Wavertree* was gale-whipped and smashed up off Cape Horn. From temporary refuge in the Falklands she was sold off and towed away to Punta Arenas in 1911. For fifty-five years the old ship served as storage hulk and sand barge – until 'discovered' by shipping enthusiasts in 1966. Repaired and towed to New York in 1970, she was painstakingly restored ahead of her centenary, to become a historic showpiece at South Street Seaport Museum.

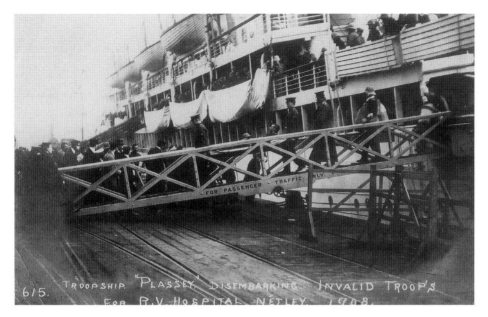

TROOPSHIP "PLASSEY" DISEMBARKING INVALID TROOP'S
FOR R.V. HOSPITAL NETLEY. 1908.
615.

Above and below: Postcard subjects for the Woolston photographer J.T. Eltringham included these 1908 scenes of invalid troops disembarking from HMT *Plassy* at Southampton docks, to be taken by train to the Royal Victoria Hospital at Netley. In service from 1900 until scrapped in 1924, the 7,400-ton *Plassy* was one of three P & O steamers built primarily for Government contract work conveying garrison troops to and from India and other parts of the old Empire. In 1894 Southampton was designated the centre for peacetime troop movements – a significant factor in the enhancement of the port.

Many other vessels were requisitioned to take troops to and from South Africa during the Boer Wars of 1899-1902. During the First World War, 8.15 million servicemen, with associated weapons, vehicles and supplies (including 859,830 horses!) passed through Southampton.

INVALID TROOPS IN
AMBULANCE TRAIN
FOR
R.V. HOSPITAL NETLEY.
612.

In the six years from August 1914 some 2.66 million sick and wounded servicemen were brought back to Britain – over half of them to Southampton, whence special ambulance trains dispersed them to hospitals around the country. A total of 7,882 such journeys were recorded, about 1,200 of them to Netley.

The Royal Victoria Hospital, for which Queen Victoria laid the foundation stone on 19 May 1856, was built in response to the medical disasters of the Crimean War – albeit Florence Nightingale's ideas of good hospital planning were put second to achieving architectural splendour, as nicely displayed in this Edwardian postcard by the ubiquitous F.G.O. Stuart. Opened in 1863, the first British purpose-built military hospital contained over 1,000 beds in 138 wards, arranged behind a frontage 468 yards long.

From 1900 the RVH had its own branch railway line and station, to which patients were conveyed in special 'Netley coaches' from Southampton docks. The hospital pier, which did not extend to deep water, was a useful recreational facility for men recuperating, as illustrated in this Stuart postcard first issued during the First World War.

During the Boer War RVH accommodation was doubled by huts and tents erected behind the main building. In the First World War what was styled British Red Cross Hospital No. 1 similarly added 1,500 beds in temporary premises. Altogether about 50,000 sick and wounded men passed through Netley in 1914-19.

The RVH also played an important role in The Second World War but in the 1950s its buildings mostly became disused. The main block was demolished in 1966, except the chapel which is now the centre of the Royal Victoria Country Park, created in 1980 by Hampshire County Council after it had acquired the RVH site and extensive grounds.

First World War patients at Netley included soldiers from various Commonwealth countries. Medical staff at the BRC Hospital were also augmented by volunteers from overseas. Noteworthy among them throughout 1915 were twenty-four Red Cross sisters and nurses from Japan; they posed for photographs outside one of the hospital huts.

Stuart found an appealing postcard subject in the 12,105-ton Royal Mail Liner *Asturias*, built by Harland & Wolff, which made her maiden Southampton – Buenos Aires voyage in May 1908. She continued running to South America until requisitioned in August 1914 as a hospital ship, to make numerous trips carrying wounded servicemen from the Mediterranean and France. Although identified by her white hull, green band and red crosses, the *Asturias* was torpedoed on 20 March 1917, near Start Point, with the loss of forty-five lives. She was beached, refloated, towed to Plymouth and used as an ammunition hulk. In 1919 Royal Mail reclaimed her from the Admiralty and had her rebuilt at Belfast. Renamed *Arcadian*, she ran cruises from 1923 until laid up in 1930.

Among the subjects of the shipping postcard issued during the First World War from the Oxford Street bookshop of Miss G.A. Pratt was the *Jan Breydel*. This 1,767-ton steamer was one of four Belgian government mail ships used as ambulance transports and hospital ships under British command in 1914-19.

About 1912 F.G.O. Stuart arranged with his German printers to provide postcards publicising the paddle steamers of the Southampton, Isle of Wight and South of England RMSP Company – more manageably known as Red Funnel. Among them was the 326-ton *Princess Mary*, built in 1911 by Day, Summers & Company at Northam. She was one of sixteen Red Funnel ships taken for wartime duty as patrol vessels and minesweepers, mostly in the Mediterranean. *Princess Mary* survived the war but was lost on 2 August 1919 when her hull was ripped open by submerged wreckage of HMS *Majestic*, which had been mined during the Dardanelles operations.

Stuart also issued cards depicting Union Castle and Royal Mail vessels serving as wartime hospital ships. One of a dozen requisitioned 'Castle' ships was the *Braemar Castle*, of 6,266 tons, built in 1898. She survived striking a mine in the Aegean Sea on 23 November 1916 and later served as a base hospital off Murmansk and Archangel during British intervention against Bolshevik Russia in 1918-19. With decks boarded in to counter the intense cold, she was nicknamed 'Noah's Ark'. She resumed Union Castle services to South Africa from 1919 until withdrawn for scrapping in 1924.

Among the seventy-seven vessels commissioned as military hospital and ambulance transport ships in the First World War were three of the largest liners – *Britannic*, *Mauretania* and *Aquitania*. The latter, a 45,647-ton Cunarder, served briefly in 1914 as an armed merchant cruiser, then as a hospital ship in 1915-17. On one voyage from the Dardanelles she brought nearly 5,000 wounded to Southampton; twenty ambulance trains were needed to take them to various hospitals. The *Aquitania* next became a troopship; on 19 May 1919 she left Southampton carrying 5,400 soldiers home to Canada, before returning to start her first Cunard voyage from Southampton to New York on 14 June 1919. Thereafter, this popular liner maintained a long association with Southampton until withdrawn for scrapping at the end of 1949.

This Stuart card depicted RMS *Homeric*, which made her maiden voyage from Southampton to New York in February 1922. Launched at Danzig in 1913 as the *Columbus* for the NDL Line, this 34,351-ton vessel was among those taken over by the Allies. She was completed for use by the White Star Line.

One of the last Stuart cards (no. 2158 in his main series ending with 2181) offered this view of four great liners in the Ocean Dock around 1922, exemplifying their heyday between the Wars when Southampton was justifiably styled 'The Gateway to the World'.

At the left is the *Homeric*, which shared White Star transatlantic services within the *Majestic* and *Olympic* for ten years up to 1932; thereafter she ran only pleasure cruises, until sold for scrapping in 1936. The 45,324-ton *Olympic* (shown sailing, at left centre) was more fortunate than her sister ships *Titanic* and *Britannic*. The first of this trio built by Harland & Wolff at Belfast, she made her maiden voyage from Southampton to New York in June 1911. After being extensively rebuilt for increased safety following the *Titanic* disaster, she was taken over as a troopship from August 1914. Dubbed 'Old Reliable', she carried over 200,000 servicemen on voyages totalling some 180,000 miles, before resuming scheduled services from Southampton in July 1920. These were continued until April 1935, when she was laid up there and later sold for scrapping.

Between the *Olympic* and the *Aquitania* (far right) Stuart's photograph features the *Berengaria*. Originally the HAPAG liner *Imperator*, built at Hamburg, she was then the world's largest at 52,226 tons; she was accorded a civic welcome when first calling at Southampton in June 1913. Her German voyages ceased on the outbreak of war, during which she was kept in port at Hamburg.

Taken by the Allies, she was acquired in 1920 by Cunard, which renamed her and had her converted to oil fuel. With the *Aquitania* and *Mauretania*, the *Berengaria* made a noteworthy threesome on Atlantic crossings during the inter-War years. Her final voyage from Southampton was made in March 1938, after which she went for scrap.

Postscript

The last of the pre-war HAPAG liners, the *Vaterland* called at Southampton in 1914, before being interned that August at New York, to become an American troopship in 1917. Taken as reparations and allocated to the United States Lines, refitted and renamed *Leviathan*, she ran transatlantic services from July 1923 until withdrawn in September 1934.

The great Christmas party given by her crew to 800 needy Southampton schoolchildren – subject of a Pathé newsreel photograph reproduced in *Southampton, The Second Selection*, page 76 – can now be dated as 12 December 1923 and the man leading them in the arduous role of Father Christmas identified, thanks to his granddaughter. He was the liner's head chef, Richard Pearse (1877-1950), who spent his working life on various liners, becoming well known to celebrities travelling aboard them.

Other local titles published by Tempus

Southampton, The Second Selection
A.G.K. LEONARD

This compilation of over 220 photographs and other images document the many aspects of social history and development of Southampton from Victorian times to the Second World War. They recall bygone townscapes, transport and shipping scenes, past occupations, occasions and recreations, and some of the people who made their distinctive contributions to the growth of the town and port

0 7524 2484 X

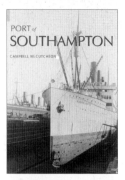

Port of Southampton
CAMPBELL McCUTCHEON

Sheltered by the Isle of Wight, Southampton has for centuries been a trading port. It was in 1838 that expansion of the port from a small series of wharfs began in earnest. Still under development today, the Port of Southampton grew to be the biggest passenger port in the UK. This collection of photographs will hopefully bring back memories of Southampton's port to those who have sailed through or worked there.

0 7524 3268 0

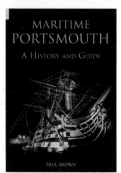

Maritime Portsmouth, A History and Guide
PAUL BROWN

For three centuries Portsmouth has been the leading base of the Royal Navy, although its history as a port can be traced back to Roman times. From the Roman walls at Portchester to the best-preserved Georgian dockyard in the world, and HMS *Victory* the most illustrious survivor from the sailing navy, Portsmouth can lay claim to being the most important naval site in the UK and, perhaps, the world. Certainly, no other dockyard can claim to be as complete and to have as varied a selection of buildings.

0 7524 3537 X

Haunted Winchester
MATTHEW FELDWICK

Drawing on historical and contemporary sources *Haunted Winchester* contains a chilling range of ghostly accounts. This selection includes tales of spectral monks at Winchester Cathedral and phantom horses in the Cathedral Close, as well as stories of the Eclipse Inn where Dame Alice Lisle, condemned by Judge Jefferies, still walks. This phenomenal gathering of ghostly goings-on is bound to captivate anyone interested in the supernatural history of the area.

0 7524 3846 8

If you are interested in purchasing other books published by Tempus, or in case you have difficulty finding any Tempus books in your local bookshop, you can also place orders directly through our website

www.tempus-publishing.com